*Georgian*
*Delights*

To William and Lesley

# *GEORGIAN DELIGHTS*

J. H. PLUMB

Weidenfeld & Nicolson
London
M.CM.LXXX

ISBN 0 297 77720

Designed by Sara Komar
Picture Editor Julia Brown
House Editor Wendy Dallas

Filmset and printed in Great Britain
by BAS Printers Limited, Over Wallop, Hampshire

FRONTISPIECE
William Hogarth *The Happy Marriage: The Masked Ball at Wanstead*
[detail].

# *CONTENTS*

# *AUTHOR'S ACKNOWLEDGMENT*

I am indebted to Edmund Pillsbury of the Yale Center for British Art for permission to use material from the catalogue of *The Pursuit of Happiness* exhibition which marked the opening of this remarkable gift to Yale by Mr Paul Mellon. During the early stages of planning that exhibition I was helped by many scholars but above all by Professor Jules Prown with whom it was a delight to work. I am also grateful to the Yale Center for their permission to use reproductions of so many of the pictures, drawings and engravings in their custody – one of the richest stores in the world of British eighteenth-century art.

I also owe a debt to my former research assistants who helped me over a much larger project of which this book is an early sampling – David Vincent, Andrew Parkinson and Peter Oborne – and also my colleague Joachim Whaley. And it has been a delight to work with the editorial staff of Weidenfeld and Nicolson.

J. H. Plumb

# PART ONE

*The Pursuit of Happiness*

Increasingly from the last quarter of the seventeenth century in Britain there was a change in man's attitude to himself and to the world about him. Men and women felt that happiness was to be found on earth as well as in heaven, that the works of a bountiful creator were to be enjoyed, not shunned. Indeed, this attitude strengthened so powerfully that Thomas Jefferson embodied in the Declaration of Independence the pursuit of happiness as an inalienable natural right, on the same terms as liberty and life. Even if enshrined as a social goal, happiness, alas, is often elusive and usually expensive in its pursuit. It can, of course, be achieved without money, but the ecstatic happiness of a hair-shirted saint had little appeal for men and women of the eighteenth century. They were religious, certainly, often with a deep sincerity rather than mere conviction, but their religion was socially orientated. They felt a need to reconcile their increasingly powerful desire to enjoy the fruits of creation and the world about them with a sense of moral purpose. Happiness could not be derived from license, nor from dissipation, nor from idleness. Happiness was deepest when linked with self-improvement, either through the social arts or through the enjoyment of nature in all its manifestations – not only its beauties, but also its secrets – for where else was the purpose as well as the goodness of God the creator to be found?

For the men, women and children of eighteenth-century England, at least those beyond the borders of poverty, the world became increasingly radiant. There were more things to possess, more activities – intellectual, artistic and sporting – to enjoy; the passions of the mind, the heart and the body could be more easily and more socially indulged. 'More socially' is important to stress: happiness became less private, less a state of the soul, a personal relationship with God, than something visible to one's neighbours. The pursuit of happiness was entangled in social emulation; it therefore became competitive; and competition requires money and time as well as desire.

Fortunately the art of eighteenth-century England will not allow us to forget how delightful the world had become to those who had the means to enjoy it. In paintings, in watercolours, in drawings, in prints and panoramas and in vividly illustrated books, their new happiness found full recognition. Few pictures radiate with such a powerful sense of happiness as Francis Wheatley's brilliant painting *Family Group in a Landscape* (see jacket), or convey so fully the pleasures of the eighteenth-century gentry: firstly there is the romantic landscape, perhaps created by the husband, or improved by him in order to delight the eye; even more important is the implied happiness of the husband and wife with their children – ordinary to us, yet marking a vital social change in eighteenth-century life. In the seventeenth century upper-class children had spent little time with their parents, who were concerned to maintain an oppressive patriarchal authority, but in the art of the late eighteenth century we find children everywhere – making music, sketching, riding, visiting ruins, picnicking with their parents – sharing with them the pleasures of the mind, the body and the heart. In one vivid scene Wheatley encapsulates the new world of family happiness.

The art of the eighteenth century brings us the sense of freshness and delight that infused so many of the activities of eighteenth-century men and women. What, to us, is commonplace – a concert, a play, a ball, a race meeting, or even travel for travel's sake – was to them exciting and *new*, activities which they knew their fathers and grandfathers had never, or at the least rarely, enjoyed.

The late seventeenth and early eighteenth centuries witnessed a revolution in availability of information, in movement, and, most important of all, a growth of affluence amongst the middle and upper-middle classes. These factors interacted with each other to

George Morland *The Tea Garden*, c. 1790.

generate what can only be described as a cultural revolution: more and more men and women enjoyed leisure and possessed the means to fill their time with purposeful activity. For this revolution in the social life of Britain in the eighteenth century there was no single causative factor – no trigger that released change, and so moved society into a higher gear, as a clutch does a motor engine. There were obvious economic factors – growth of population, agricultural revolution, improved food supply, technological inventions, availability of cheap money, expanding home and foreign markets, the factory system, and the division of labour for mass production – all of which have been held responsible at one time or another, either singly or together, for the transformation of English society from the world of agriculture and craftsmanship to that of industry. What are so frequently, one might say unfortunately, omitted from any discussion of one of the most momentous changes ever achieved in social living are the will, the desires, the ambitions, and the cravings of the men and women who wanted change and promoted it.

Realizing that there was a market in culture, men of business began quite deliberately to exploit it, to expand it, and to pursue innovation and sophistication in order to reap the profits that were there. This entrepreneurial spirit can be found amongst the great artists such as William Hogarth, who exploited contemporary excitements with a quickly executed print; the booksellers such as John Newbery, who extended the market in children's literature; the racing men like O'Kelley, the owner of Eclipse, the first racehorse to bring a fortune to his owner, down to the makers of educational toys or cheap musical instruments, and the itinerant lecturers who battened on the culture-hungry provincial towns. They were all bent on teasing guineas from purses that would willingly open for any cultural activity which would both delight and improve. Particularly *improve*, for happiness was not likely to be engendered by mere entertainment, but only if leisure were well spent, and either the mind, the body or the heart exercised and improved. Happiness was quite distinct from dissipation, even if, at times, the borderline became blurred.

Money was fundamental to happiness. The great world wars of the eighteenth century, in which Britain crushed France's imperial aspirations, invigorated commerce and industry within Britain, as well as bringing the riches of Africa, the West Indies, North America and India within its tentacles. In spite of great fluctuations and recurring depressions, the rich became richer and so did the middle classes; even many working-class families enjoyed an income sufficient to enable them to participate in a modest way in the expanding world of leisure – to saunter in the new pleasure gardens, to take their children to the circus, to gaze at the elaborate panoramas of foreign cities which, with mechanical and scientific wonders, drew large audiences in London and the provinces. All of these helped to create the atmosphere of a new and exciting world, one which was a delight to explore as well as enjoy. Such an attitude permeates the culture of the eighteenth century, whether it be the vivid and picturesque adventures of Tom Jones, or Dr Johnson and Boswell stomping about the Hebrides, or Loutherbourg's revellers alive with joy as they rattle away in a coach.

Movement – by comparison with all that went before – became easy and cheap in eighteenth-century England, and the horse and coach brought as much happiness as the automobile does today, and far less pollution. Although the horse had been domesticated for millenia and used for agriculture as well as war, travel and sport, the eighteenth century and the early nineteenth were to be its greatest age, and it is not ridiculous to maintain that there was a veritable horse revolution starting around 1700. They were bred and adapted for rapid travel. Coaches and carriages were constantly refined to attain higher speeds. The horse population grew prodigiously, since horses were reasonably cheap and could therefore be consumed with equanimity in the arduous and killing work of dragging coaches at high speeds. But the horse was more than a machine. It possessed great aesthetic qualities and, when carefully bred, immense versatility. The huge shire horses – the Clydesdales and Suffolk Punches – were vast engines of power that could plough deep or haul great farm wagons. The racehorse, however, which was steadily improved by the importation not only of the great Arab stallions – Lord Godolphin Arabian, the Byerly Turk and the Darby Arabian – but also, and more importantly, of Arab mares, became fleeter and fleeter and more beautiful and elegant. The coach horse had to be both fast and strong, and its stamina capable of lasting the usual twenty miles of a stage; for this purpose the Cleveland Bay was regarded as the best horse, and its fame was so great that Hull exported droves of them – even to countries as distant as Poland. The horse, the carriage and the new swift movement provided ecstatic delight as well as exhilaration; indeed, the horse became an object of intense veneration, its beauty exploited in countless pictures. From John Wootton onwards there was a growing rage for horse painting that reaches its zenith in the remarkable studies of George Stubbs, who was as much obsessed by the horse as were his patrons. In fact he spent days in the putrid atmosphere of a decaying horse, carefully dissecting it layer by layer and drawing its anatomy with a precision never before achieved. Although his horses were therefore more exact, he always infused them with nobility, splendour and grace. And it is not surprising that in some of Stubbs's pictures there are the light phaetons, the delicate chaises, which matched the elegance and speed of his horses. And it was not only the aristocracy and the gentry who wished their horses to be immortalized in paint. By 1780 most provincial towns of any consequence possessed a horse painter who would do a likeness in oils for two or three guineas. The period 1700–1840 was the true age of the horse, not only as the motive power behind the growing affluence of England but as the mechanism that engendered happiness and the diffusion of culture.

The revolution in transport was comparable to that of our own age. By 1700 major towns were already linked by a stage-coach service to London, but there was rarely more than one a week, and the journeys were arduous, slow, fraught with danger and often impossible for long periods of the winter. During this century, roads, like the horse and coach, also improved, at first slowly, then dramatically, to meet the demand for faster and more frequent travel. By 1800 all towns south of the Trent and east of the Severn were within a comfortable day's journey from London, whereas in 1700 it had taken three days to reach the city from Southampton. Even in 1754 it took four and a half days to get from Manchester to

Thomas Rowlandson *The Canterbury to Dover Coach.*

London, but by 1825 it could be done most days of the year in eighteen hours. By that time there were forty coaches daily on the London–Brighton run, packed high with passengers and luggage, indeed often filled with businessmen visiting their families for the weekend. Travel was in a constant process of improvement, spurred by intense competition and rivalry, of which speed was the essence. Hence we can feel some of the excitement that gripped the passengers, immortalized for us in the canvases of James Pollard, who was obsessed by the poetry of coaching.

This revolution in travel, the comparative ease, comfort and speed with which one could move about England by the last quarter of the eighteenth century, is profoundly important – not merely for its influence on economic development, but also because of the changes it encouraged in the style of life: not only people travelled in increasing numbers along the English roads, but so did fashions and ideas. Salesmen, musicians, actors, circuses, lecturers on science and philosophy, drawing masters, fencing masters, teachers of language, conjurors, magicians and firework engineers were on the move, bringing variety and novelty and metropolitan sophistication to replace provincial isolation. It is difficult to capture the excitement of these changes – the way they seized the public imagination. Nevertheless, the most vital catalyst carried by the rattling coach – the provincial newspaper – was more humble and so aesthetically dreary that it rarely appears in a picture.

With the lapsing of the licensing act in 1695, press censorship virtually came to an end in Britain, permitting the establishment of newspapers, first in London and subsequently in the provinces. By 1760 London possessed morning and evening papers, and several that were published twice or thrice weekly. Only on Sunday were Londoners without a daily paper. By 1780 the provincial press had rooted itself in all the major towns of Britain, so that no family which could afford twopence need fail to have a weekly newspaper delivered. Newspapers, indeed, were often cheaper, and in London they were published for as little as a farthing. No country in the world possessed so complex or so widespread a newspaper system, which played a most vital part in the cultural development of England in the eighteenth and early nineteenth centuries. As important as the news which these papers carried were the advertisements, which give us fascinating evidence of the growing pursuit of happiness in all of its remarkable diversity; for the newspapers not only spread knowledge of race-meetings, concerts, theatres, assemblies, balls and lectures, but they also excited the imagination, whetted the appetite and enticed people to leave their firesides, to get into their coaches or astride their horses in order to participate in the expanding world of culture.

Better roads, more horses, finer coaches, and information about what was happening were the foundations upon which cultural growth could take place, permitting men and women of modest affluence to move more freely and purposefully about their world. And the greatest delight they discerned was often their own country, including its riches of landscape and antiquities.

The English in the eighteenth century developed the idea of a holiday associated with travel, an activity which has subsequently spread to the four corners of the earth and brought happiness to millions. Holidays, of course, existed before, but for most people they were associated with religious ritual or the dramatic moments of the sun's year. They took place within the community – the town or village or guild. Sometimes they were associated with solemn occasions of a human life – the marriage of princes, the death of a ruler, the celebration of victory. And those who worked in the orbits of power might travel from capital to capital, from court to court; but what was extremely rare was for a man or a woman or a family to go off on their travels just for the fun of it or to indulge themselves by visiting the world about them. And it took a very long time for men

Front page of *The Weekly Journal: or, British Gazetteer*, 13 May 1721.

( 1515 )
THE
Weekly Journal:
OR,
British Gazetteer.

Lucifer's new Row-Barge for First-Rate Passengers.

and women to free themselves from a sense of guilt and to travel, as it were, without a moral purpose. So the origin of holiday travel, and indeed the beginnings of towns devoted almost entirely to leisure, were rooted in health, for the leisure towns of eighteenth-century Britain were the spas – Bath, Scarborough, Buxton and the rest.

People in the eighteenth century were prone to a host of minor ailments – particularly skin diseases and rheumatism – due to unbalanced diet, overcrowded housing and excessive clothing necessary for ill-warmed houses and coaches. Furthermore, food was extremely cheap and, amongst the middle classes, overeating so much a commonplace of life that the huge, fat men and women were a popular target for the satire of a Gilray or a Rowlandson. And the medical profession, as well as their patients, believed passionately in the value of the purge. On a fine day, at the crack of dawn, crowds of men and women would leave London on foot, on horse or in a coach, flocking to Epsom Downs, there to take the strong purgative waters that acted with dramatic alacrity and sent the men and women hastening to their own tract of bushes. The rich, however, with time on their hands, preferred a more leisurely and a more genteel procedure. They hacked down the Great West Road to Bath, whose hot chalybeate springs had been discovered by the Romans and remained in use, particularly for barren women, ever after. It was only in the late seventeenth century, however, that taking the waters at Bath began to be transformed into an occasion for social delights. When card-sharpers, ladies of the town and widows looking for husbands soon followed the sick and the not so sick, Bath became a boisterous town. It was cleaned up in Queen Anne's reign by 'Beau' Nash, the Master of Ceremonies, who not only abolished riding boots, swords and aprons, and insisted vigorously on genteel behaviour, but introduced music, encouraged the theatre, turned dances into balls, beautified the Pump Room, yet permitted – indeed, encouraged – gambling, and tolerated intrigue so long as it was discreet. And so within ten years Bath became the summer colony of the beau monde, the home of heads of fashion, who drew crowds in their wake. Old Bath was torn down and the Bath which we know, one of the loveliest of all towns in Europe, was built – its squares and crescents and terraces all in the great tradition of classical architecture. Indeed, there are few cities in the world which reflect an age so completely as Bath, or more accurately the eighteenth-century attitude to life – its charm, its wit, its never-ending delight in the physical world.

Bath spawned a host of imitators. Near London was Tunbridge

Aquatint by J. C. Nattes *The Pump Room, Bath*, 1805.

Wells, easy to visit for a few days or a long weekend, as well as Cheltenham and Leamington in the West Midlands; but the list is endless, for even by the 1730s there were hundreds of spas in England alone, a majority of them boasting a hotel as well as curative waters.

Fortunately, Dr Russell of Brighton in the 1740s decided that bathing in and drinking hot or cold sea water was immensely beneficial to the health. And so sea bathing began in a tentative way. It was the patronage of Weymouth by King George III, and of Brighton by his son the Prince Regent, which helped the birth of the seaside resort, particularly the latter, who built himself a strange exotic house there – half pavilion, half oriental palace – in which to indulge his pursuits both aesthetic and amorous. Brighton was perfectly placed – a day's drive from London. It also faced south, protected on the north by the rolling Downs, which were ideal not only for horse-racing but also for watching the light phaetons race one against the other, or even for holding exercises of the militia in which the rich young bloods could indulge their passion for extravagant uniforms and beautiful horses. The middle classes followed the rich, and soon one classical terrace after another was stretching down the coastline from the Pavilion, making Brighton almost as beautiful as Bath, and certainly capturing the spirit of life in fashionable Regency England; indeed, the transition from a health resort to a town designed for leisure and pleasure came more quickly in Brighton than elsewhere in the country. It was the world's first Miami, built fortunately in an age of exceptional architectural judgement. Brighton's success led to a string of tiny fishing villages on the Channel coast mushrooming into elegant seaside resorts – Margate, Sidmouth, Lyme Regis, Weymouth. There the gentry and the middle classes learned the delights of sea bathing, but they also found other pleasures to which they were addicted – assemblies, balls and races, and also the quieter pleasures of the mind, whether it was improving their collections of fossils or reading the latest books from the circulating libraries.

The ease of travel must not be exaggerated: coaches could overturn (John Wesley nearly drowned on the Great North Road); highwaymen were as ubiquitous as gnats; the bitter elements of driving rain or freezing fog bred drunken coachmen, and so frequent disaster; many inns were utterly deplorable, and beds shared with strangers were common even at the end of the century. Yet such was the novelty, such the delight in the discovery of Britain, that the number of travellers steadily increased, travelling purely for the sake of travelling, out to discover a landscape of varied beauty and a British past that still littered the land – castles, ruined abbeys, the strange stones of the Druids, as well as the industrial novelties of their own age.

Landscape for its own sake – to delight the eye, to bring solemnity and enchantment to the mind, or to be seen in terms of the human

Etching by George Cruikshank *Beauties of Brighton*, 1826.

heart or human destiny – developed strongly only in the second half of the century. Earlier travellers took delight, like Defoe, in acres of ripening corn, in the crowded harbours that declared England's prosperity; barren and mountainous lands were regarded as bleak obstacles to the traveller, irritating and nothing more. Sir Harbottle Grimston thought Wales 'dreary' in 1768, and was pleased to get out of Snowdonia. Ten years later mountains were all the rage. Wales became 'magnificent, striking, superb', a smaller Switzerland. As with Switzerland, travellers admired the small farmers living lives of simple austerity that possessed a singular harmony with nature in contrast with the corruptions and vices of the sophisticated society of London. The fertile valleys, with their honest peasants, began to echo like a theme song in the diaries of travel, as did the sense of awe, wonder and challenge created by the highest of Welsh mountains, Snowdon. Increasingly, men and women accepted that challenge, so that a climb to its summit became the climax of a Welsh tour; up they went in the most improbable of clothes – billowing skirts and lace bonnets, frock coats and tricorne hats; terror-struck by precipices, ladies fainted and swooned (it was expected of them!). The summit achieved ('the sublime of terror', they called it), they revived themselves not by drinking brandy but by washing their faces in it – a necessary protection, it would seem, of the facial muscles that might be affected by height! It is not surprising that painters were soon immortalizing what was so keenly enjoyed, both in Wales and further north in the Lake District. As the *Monthly Magazine* wrote in 1778, 'To *make the Tour* of the Lakes, to speak in fashionable language is the *ton* of the present hour.' By 1790 the lakes and mountains were steadily being commercialized as crowds of visitors from the Midlands and London swept in. Summer houses were built at places giving the more picturesque views; guides at five shillings a day abounded; steps were cut on rocky ascents; alpine bridges were thrown over mountain streams; pleasure boats roamed the lakes, letting off brass cannon at rocky points noted for their echo, or dropping anchor whilst a concert of French horns exploited the acoustics more dexterously.

Such delights demanded repetition, and the adventurous, satiated with Wales and the Lakes, took to Scotland. What had once been a remarkable adventure for Dr. Johnson and Boswell became the well-trodden route of southern holidaymakers, bent on the sublime and the picturesque. Enjoyment of landscape and storm, vistas of mountain, sea and sky, were established as a part of life's keenest pleasures for those who had the money to travel. And, back home,

Philippe de Loutherbourg *View of Snowdon from Capel Curig*, 1787.

naturally they wished to stir their memories or bore their neighbours, so they bought landscapes – in paint, watercolour or print. Hence from 1780 until well into the nineteenth century there was a great surge in the publication of beautifully illustrated books relating to travel in Great Britain.

As they made towards Wales or the Lake District, or pushed up into Scotland, they came across the vestiges of England's past. To many the vast castles of Conway or Caernarvon, the massive, crumbling remains of Hadrian's Wall, the sad, remote ruins of Fountains Abbey or Tintern were new experiences, their first acquaintance with the visible remains of ages long past. Particularly was this true of those who lived in the new cities of the Midlands and the North – Birmingham, Manchester or Sheffield. These ruins brought to them a sense of belonging to an ancient land whose roots stretched back to the strange world of the Druids. They bought avidly the books of prints which often were available at the ruin itself, to relive their experience on their return. Many based their excursions on visiting antiquities, often plundering them for relics with which to decorate the Gothic follies which they built in their own gardens. The past they searched for was a romantic past, not a scholarly one; even the best of antiquarians, such as William Stukely, manufactured myths about Stonehenge and Avebury with the ease of a poet. Composed of myth and fable, often as bogus as Ossian, nevertheless the past brought a sense of tradition and continuity to the changing world of eighteenth-century England.

The living proved as exciting as the dead. It is hard for us to realize that the great houses of eighteenth-century England – Blenheim, Stowe, Petworth, Houghton, Holkham and many more in every county – were extremely modern to English men and women, even though the principles upon which they were built reached back to the Renaissance and then to Rome. And viewing such houses was a part of summer travel, not only for dilettantes such as Horace Walpole, who meticulously planned his summer jaunts to take in as many houses as possible, but also for many ordinary men and women, such as Mrs Libbye Powys who would have faded into total oblivion except that she wrote up her country-house visiting. Then, as now, there was a fee for entry – usually paid to the housekeeper; and most of the tours were conducted ones, as at Holkham. Often there could be a long wait in the lobby whilst earlier parties were dealt with. It was the modernity of the arrangements, as well as the pictures and furnishings, which entranced the visitors. Few, for example, came away from Houghton in Norfolk without commenting on its exceptional convenience and the profusive use of the novel West Indian wood – mahogany.

Yet for the eighteenth-century traveller modernity had another aspect. The new factories, with their strong indication of the British future of growth and prosperity, were found every bit as exciting as the ruins or the country houses. On the way to the Lakes or to Wales, travellers would turn aside to visit the new pottery works of Josiah Wedgwood at Etruria, or the Soho works of Boulton and Watt at Birmingham, which produced every kind of metal goods from steam engines to shoe buckles, and where they might easily glimpse more exalted visitors – a German margrave, a French duke, or even a member of the royal family. Many preferred industrial sights which, like the mountains themselves, provoked a sense of awe – a flaming forge that looked like Hell, or the dangerous descent of a coal or copper mine; equally fashionable were the huge salt mines of Cheshire, although one tourist did admit that it 'requires a good strong stomach, and a large portion of curiosity to go through with this'. Curiosity was great and stomachs strong, and women as well as men sat in tiny baskets hanging on the end of rope and chain, to be lowered several hundred feet into the bowels of the earth – dank, malodorous and very dark. No wonder they tended to burst into 'Rule Britannia' and 'God Save the King' when they made the surface again! The most popular of all industrial sites was Coalbrookdale, which was close to Birmingham yet on the way to

Wales, and possessed not only coal mines and iron forges but the first iron bridge to be constructed by man – three wonders for the price of one. In Joseph Wright of Derby England produced a painter who could convey the awesome poetry that infused the new industrialism, at least in the eyes of its contemporary beholders.

A short yearly visit to a spa or the seaside, usually for two weeks, interspersed with an occasional journey to more distant places, was quite as much as even the prosperous middle-class traveller could afford, yet the world beyond Britain developed a stronger and stronger magnetic pull for the aristocracy. Visits to France, above all to Italy, and sometimes to the rest of Europe, even to lands as distant as Russia and Greece, had come to be regarded as essential in forming the taste and acquiring the polish of a gentleman.

Indeed, the flow of young men, with their tutors and servants, had become so large by the 1760s that the structure of modern travel gradually came into existence – printed guidebooks containing maps, road conditions, money and conversion tables; phrase books in every language; coach-hire systems; lists of recommended hotels; couriers; foreign exchange facilities; and specialized guides to beauty spots. There were no cameras, it is true, but if rich enough, as, say, was William Beckford, then one took along a watercolourist – in his case, J. R. Cozens – or hired a local artist, as did William Wyndham, who employed Busoni. These artists and others immortalized the scenes that were to enliven the walls of many a mansion in Britain. If one was less affluent, there were always the racks of prints – plain or coloured and very cheap – of famous cities, historical monuments or well-known beauty spots.

The Grand Tour usually began at Calais, where innkeepers were rapacious, the huckstering endless and the confusion bewildering; for those who took their own coaches and servants the dangers of Calais were far less than for those forced to hire them. In fact, the first lesson that a young gentleman learned was his pocket's vulnerability. Usually the travellers did not make straight for Paris, but went off with their tutors to a provincial city to learn the language. They were thought to be too young to encounter the sophistications of Paris, although most fathers expected – indeed, hoped – that during their tour the young men would learn the arts of love as well as foreign languages; the Earl of Pembroke even went so far as to recommend his former mistress to his son. Ultimately, however, they went to Paris to learn the arts of social living, to buy the luxury goods which were so much more sumptuous than those to be found in England, and to appraise the architecture, for the

Pompeo Battoni *William Gordon*, painted in Rome, 1766.

criticism of buildings was a necessary attribute of a polished man of the world. But Paris was never the final goal of the tourists; that was Italy, and, above all, Rome. As Dr Johnson said, 'A man who has not been in Italy is always conscious of an inferiority.' In Rome they became *cognoscenti*. There were a number of expatriates who acted as guides, art dealers and cicerones of all trades. Italy was the land of marvels, the antique shop of Europe. Young Englishmen were expected to return festooned with works of art. So beady-eyed entrepreneurs ransacked palaces, abbeys and convents, employed spies and informers, and on occasion were not above manufacturing fakes. And, of course, to satisfy the market, Italians burrowed like wombats into the ashes of Pompeii or the graveyards of the Campania to secure objects for sale. The young aristocrats, whether artistically inclined or not, were taught to revere not only the arts but also the past which enshrined them, and so the classical heritage became a vital force in their lives, influencing the houses they built, the shape of the urns with which they adorned their terraces, and the colours they used to paint their walls. And they saw themselves as the heirs of a great tradition. The experience provided by Italy was as much as the majority of tourists desired or could afford, either in time or money; so their knowledge of antiquities was largely confined to Rome, apart perhaps from a glimpse of the Greek temples at Paestum. But the world beyond Italy always beckoned a few bolder spirits, and naturally drew to it architects and artists who wished not only to savour the antiquities of Greece but also to draw closer to the very foundations of European art and culture. Hence the travels of 'Athenian' Stuart and Nicholas Revett to Greece or the visit of Richard Wood and James Dawkins to Palmyra. This was not, of course, wandering for wandering's sake but the determined pursuit of forms and style and decorative material.

As the British established themselves in distant and exotic lands, impecunious artists or those with a hunger for travel saw the opportunity of new markets, the chance to paint the factories of the East India Company in Calcutta or the merchants at Canton; maybe also to sell them genre scenes, as did Brunias in the West Indies, or to bring their watercolours back, as did the Daniells, to adorn the beautifully printed and illustrated travel books for which the eighteenth-century gentleman had an insatiable thirst. A library was an essential feature for those who had any pretentions to civility. Rich young men were taught to revere books, for the education of young gentlemen on the Grand Tour was never merely visual or aesthetic or manly, it was also studious. They were encouraged to read modern masters as well as ancient classics. By the 1770s the intellectual excitements of the Enlightenment were as much a matter for discussion amongst the English as amongst the French. And if a man or woman's happiness lay in books, a feast awaited them.

Nothing, perhaps, created such a diversity of delight or opened so many routes to happiness in the eighteenth century as the vast growth in the publication of books and their ready availability. The seventeenth century seems rich in books and yet it was not so. Mainly they were large – folios and quartos – expensive and considerably limited in the range of subjects they covered in depth. If one's interest had been stirred by China in 1650 it could not have been satisfied, for there were hardly any books on the subject. If one wanted a cheap book to teach oneself the flute, there was none. There was no catalogue of trees and plants upon which one could browse for an afternoon; no colouring books to occupy the nursery-bound child; no large encyclopedia for quick reference or to settle a wager; hardly a newspaper; no magazines, and certainly no *Ladies Diary*, that quaint magazine with its curious mixture of mathematical problems, marital difficulties, romantic love stories and domestic science, with which to while away an hour. (Yet the *Ladies Diary* holds the record for Britain's longest lived magazine: it ran from 1704 to 1871!) And there were no circulating libraries from which to borrow the latest novel; in fact, there were scarcely any novels to read: old romances, a few picaresque novels such as *Don Quixote*, and little else.

All that changed. Books, newspapers, magazines, plays, ballads and chapbooks proliferated, so that books of every variety were available at a price within the compass not only of the middle class man and woman but also of the artisan. Delightfully illustrated children's books, such as *Jack Dandy's Delights*, could be purchased for a halfpenny. Controversial pamphlets about politics or religion could be bought for sixpence or a shilling. The same price, however, covered a multitude of books for self-teaching or even whole histories and encyclopedias if bought in parts. And for those with a few guineas to spend, literature, science, travel, religion, archaeology, poetry and belles lettres were available. The eighteenth century was a 'picture-loving age', and publishers soon found that a huge market for books, so long as the text was accompanied by beautiful coloured plates, awaited their exploitation; books on natural history, topography and travel rapidly multiplied, and while they ensnared the purchaser through the eye, their prose whetted his curiosity.

Yet perhaps the most impressive development in literature during the eighteenth century was the rise of the novel, particularly the novel of social realism exploited by Defoe, Fielding, Richardson and a host of other writers. In their hands the novel became for the first time an immensely popular art form. Even when, as with Jonathan Wild, Heartfree or Squire Allworthy, the characters are little more than moral or immoral principles made human, the circumstances of their lives are as realistic as the author could make them. Here were no exotic or gothic worlds (they were to follow) but rather the

London, the towns and the countryside that all readers could recognize. Although Richardson opened up a new world of psychological subtlety, the dominant attraction of his novels was their vivid portrayal of contemporary society.

Most novels were quite expensive, and the demand gave a great stimulus to the circulating libraries which sprang into being in the first decades of the eighteenth century, although the bulk of every library consisted of non-fiction – works on divinity, travel, history, philosophy and science far outweighing the novel.

Circulating libraries spread very rapidly. First, as one might expect, they were set up in the fashionable spas, and afterwards in the seaside resorts; indeed, Margate possessed, by the turn of the century, a magnificent circulating library, housed in a very handsome building, and Sidmouth had a very famous one – Wallis's – which was a part of the firm that dominated the market in educational toys for children. By the late decades of the eighteenth century there was no town of the slightest consequence that did not have one – and often more than one – library. They abounded in London, which contained, even in the 1740s, very large libraries indeed – Fancourts running to over 40,000 volumes, which represented a considerable outlay of capital. They grew ever more splendid, finally culminating in libraries as sumptuous as Ackermann's, the great colour-printer of Regency days, who also used the library as a showcase for his own books.

The avidity with which men and women bought books is also illustrated by the growth of the second-hand market and by the ever-increasing numbers of serious collectors and bibliophiles. Printed catalogues of second-hand books with prices began in the 1730s, but by 1777 Booth of Norwich could issue a catalogue of 15,000 volumes. Book auctions had begun earlier than this, but they were largely confined to London or the occasional cathedral city; by 1800 they were regularly held not only at Christie's and Sotheby's but in most provincial towns, and Rowlandson's gay satire (p. 69) conveys the avidity and preoccupation of bibliophile bargain hunters.

The diversity of literature of every kind, as well as its wide dissemination and availability, certainly created fertile pastures for the inquiring mind, providing habits of study and areas of intellectual curiosity which, in previous centuries, had only been available for small élites. In consequence, there were far more books in the home. Equally important was the development in the eighteenth century of a specialized literature for children – books designed to beguile them into reading, with attractive illustrations

Ramsay Richard Reinagle *Francis Noel Clarke Mundy and his Grandson, William Mundy*, 1809.

and easy typography. Indeed, by the second half of the eighteenth century it was expected that a middle-class child could be taught to read in the home by the age of five or six. And once a child was able to read he could approach any subject, from Newtonian physics to classical mythology, in books specially written for him. The dual portrait of the Mundys (above) is symbolic of what must have been – and still is – one of the greatest pleasures of family life: a shared interest in books, spreading knowledge and ideas across the generations.

It is not surprising that an age which took so much delight in literature should be passionately addicted to the theatre; indeed, after novels, plays were most in demand at the circulating libraries. They were not only read with avidity but also acted in the home. And there was far more to read or act, for more plays were written and printed in England between 1700 and 1800 than ever before or since in a similar period of time; and more than twice as many were produced in the second half of the century as in the first. The theatre became intensely popular, and throughout the century the London theatres were constantly enlarged or renewed. By 1794, for example, Drury Lane could hold an audience of 3,611. A similar increase is seen at Covent Garden: in the 1730s the average attendance has been estimated at 14,000 a week; by the 1760s it was up to 22,000 a week and it continued to increase. With so active and so eager an audience, the great managers such as John Rich began to adopt ever more elaborate scenery, employing considerable artists such as George Lambert or Philippe J. de Loutherbourg to paint the sets for them. Elaborate machinery enabled the most spectacular effects to be achieved, including, if need be, sea battles. The last vestiges of the audience were banished from the stage, footlights were introduced, and indeed the stage became a framed living picture. In the competition for audience, the star system, born in the days of Elizabeth I, was greatly extended and enhanced, particularly by Garrick, who knew as well as any Hollywood star how to project his image, whether through discreetly placed favourable notices in the newspaper or by the spectacular Shakespeare Jubilee of 1769. The engravers were kept busy, and prints of Garrick in almost every role could be obtained for one or two shillings. Two of his most famous parts were Abel Drugger (p. 28) and Macbeth. If one preferred Garrick as a chimney ornament, statuettes of him were available in either fashionable Bow china or plain Staffordshire. Of course, Garrick knew the value to himself of the social as well as the literary world, and carefully cultivated everyone from the Duke of Devonshire to Dr Samuel Johnson. Naturally he exploited every considerable artist of his acquaintance. Hogarth, always a keen-eyed entrepreneur, and realizing the growing appetite for the theatre, had painted theatrical scenes in the early '30s; his example was quickly followed, and during Garrick's lifetime theatrical painting developed into almost as specialized a genre as landscape, history or sporting pictures; a splendid example is Hayman's *The Suspicious Husband* (p. 29). Through newspapers and pamphlets, through the gossip of the salons, through prints and pictures and statuettes, David Garrick built up an enormous following and earned for himself the image of England's greatest actor – comparable to Handel in music or Reynolds in painting.

Audiences, however, could be fickle, and they loved novelty, which the theatre managers were ever eager to exploit; music and dancing had always been a part of theatrical entertainment, but now they became very much more lavish and complex. And John Rich, who in the 1720s introduced pantomime with immediate and lasting success, certainly knew the value of diversity. He realized at once the possibilities of John Gay's *Beggars' Opera*, a light comic genre that was a curiously British invention, leading to Gilbert and Sullivan and beyond. Classical opera and ballet also established themselves as a part of the theatrical life of London.

Mezzotint by S. W. Reynold's after Zoffany's *Garrick as Abel Drugger in 'The Alchemists'*, 1825

Even more impressive perhaps was the development of the provincial theatre in eighteenth-century England. In the previous century players had to content themselves with an inn yard, a hastily erected booth or a room in the Guildhall. But in 1705 Bath built the first provincial theatre, and other cities quickly followed suit. By the middle of the century some were very commodious: Norwich's theatre could seat 1,000 in 1758, and that at York was even larger. Nor was it only the old provincial capitals that built theatres. In the smaller market towns of Lincolnshire alone there were sixteen theatres, including two in the tiny port of Boston, one built by public subscription, the other by the corporation. One of the most elegant of the smaller theatres was at Grantham, little more than a staging post on the Great North Road. Often, indeed, many inns where the old strolling players had put up with the most makeshift conditions now financed a permanent theatre, with stage, lighting facilities and green room. The provincial theatres were large enough to attract London companies or the great stars of the Georgian theatre – Garrick, Kitty Clive, Henry Woodward, Mrs Siddons and others. Although the provincial theatre became very much more sophisticated, it did not, any more than did the London theatre, destroy traditional entertainment such as the fairs, with their acrobats and slack-wire artists who thought nothing of walking down a wire from the steeple of a parish church. Bartholomew Fair – so beloved by Hogarth, with its raucous collection of sideshows, human and animal monstrosities, puppet theatre, Punch and Judy, peep shows, and conjuring in every variety, mixed higgledy-piggledy with sweetmeat stalls and cheap toy stands – was only the most spectacular of hundreds of fairs that came and went across the countryside, moving from town to town to celebrate traditional feasts. Individual artists, too, continued to travel from town to town, but increasingly they came under the control of entrepreneurs who would create a theatre of varieties – a mixture of fairs, ballad singing,

Francis Hayman *A Scene from 'The Suspicious Husband'*, 1747.

animal tricks and conjuring that was the ancestor of the Victorian music hall. The most impressive development of this kind was the invention of the circus by Philip Astley, the heart of which was the horse. (Astley's horse could dance a hornpipe or make a pot of tea, lifting the kettle from the fire with its teeth.) His son was the first man to ride two horses standing up and to dance on their bare backs as he drove them around the arena; Astley, the father, invented the circus parade as a dramatic form of advertisement, leading it on a white charger flanked by trumpeters. Although he had a permanent base at his Amphitheatre in London, Astley made a summer tour of the provinces. Also instinctively aware that it was easier for men and women of the eighteenth century to enjoy themselves if they could feel that whatever they did might lead to a little self-improvement, he carried along, amidst the animals, conjurors and trapeze artists, a chronoscope – a scientific instrument for measuring the velocity of projectiles.

Since any scientific or quasi-scientific novelty entranced the eighteenth-century public, with its immense desire for knowledge, it is not surprising that ballooning took England by storm from the moment Lunardi rose into the sky in 1784. Soon advertisements for balloons and ballooning were appearing in Bury St Edmunds, Norwich, York and Exeter, and bets of an obscene nature were being made at Brooks's about what might or might not be done in the basket. These balloons, with their bright colours and lively patterns, were an aesthetic delight as well as a novelty. Their ascents usually took place, accompanied by a firework display, in the pleasure gardens which had become an important feature of eighteenth-century life; indeed, every market town had its 'Vauxhall', named after the most successful of all pleasure gardens in London. At Vauxhall there were small discreet supper booths, girls masked and unmasked, there was music and an air of freedom and frivolity; one could saunter and look at Hogarth's and Hayman's pictures; there were fashionable balls, concerts and a diversity of pleasures of a most urbane kind. Of course, there was dissipation, and often there were complaints about the whores, but at least the atmosphere was gay and light-hearted, and, with pictures of quality and with Handel's music, not uncultured. The Pantheon in Oxford Street played a similar role to Vauxhall: it was enclosed, and its huge stove made it popular in the winter months.

In the provinces these pleasure gardens were less ambitious but equally popular: they provided usually a small collection of animals and birds, a teashop, winding walks, a bowling green, and from time to time a special feature – a set piece of fireworks, a slack-wire artist, or, after Lunardi, a balloonist. Given any public occasion – a massive British victory or a jubilee to mark twenty-five or fifty years of a monarch's reign – the English liked nothing more than to build a huge set piece in one of the royal parks to celebrate the event. These contributions, as with the monument in St James's Park to George III's fifty-year jubilee in 1810 or the Great Fort in Green Park to celebrate one hundred years of Hanoverian rule, could be extremely elaborate, drawing to them wondering crowds of Londoners and helping to generate a sense that they belonged to a society which could look to the future with confidence.

Whether at the theatre, visiting the circus, looking at a puppet show, strolling through Vauxhall or around the Pantheon, even peering eagerly at the balloon struggling to rise, one could be certain that any entertainment of the time would be accompanied by music. Although the age was highly visual, it was almost besotted by music. The growth of interest and delight in making music can be seen from the rash of festivals, clubs and subscription concerts that spread like a prairie fire across provincial England in the early eighteenth century. Music publication, music teaching and the making of musical instruments approached a mass basis. As Paul Henry Lang, the great biographer of Handel, has written, 'Towards the middle of the century almost every town, castle, University or Church had its orchestra, and many musical associations gathered for weekly musical exercises.' And yet before 1680 there had scarcely been any public concerts held in England. There had been musical publications, but editions were small; likewise, instruments were expensive and teachers of music not easily found, and there were very few cheap manuals that taught the first rudimentary steps with any instrument. Hence music in the home was largely singing to the accompaniment of a stringed instrument – the lute, or in more affluent homes, the virginals. By 1750 all that was changed because instruments were cheap: at Swalecliffe, in north Oxfordshire, the villagers clubbed together to buy a bassoon, an hautboy and a *vox humana* for £2 so that the local parish church could have its 'music'; the subscribers were very humble people – weavers, wool-combers and agricultural labourers – in fact, peasants. Instruments could be loaned as well as bought, and a harpsichord only cost half a guinea a month to hire. Scores, like instruments, became very cheap indeed, well within the compass of the skilled artisan, and the same was true of teaching: music masters, charging as little as one shilling an hour, abounded: they were to be found in droves in London and the larger towns, and every small market town had at least one. Naturally, their targets were the children of the affluent or the socially aspiring. But for those families with a natural musical aptitude it was a golden age: families could develop their own small consort, for instruments were cheap enough for the practised musician to buy a number of them and become skilled in them all. And, as in every great musical age, the human voice was everywhere to be heard – singing ballads in the street, trilling arias in the fashionable opera houses, keeping up the tradition of madrigal singing in the Academy of Ancient Music, or joining one of the numerous choirs of massed voices which were such a notable feature of this age. Handel's deeply patriotic secular music, although cast in biblical themes, stirred the heart of the country. *The Messiah* was sung over and over again in cathedrals and universities, and at times the choirs reached gargantuan proportions. In 1784 Westminster Abbey was filled with several hundred singers and instruments; the orchestra was probably one of the largest ever assembled in the history of the world; but even this was matched nearly forty years later, in 1823, when York Minster, a vast cathedral, was filled with massed choirs brought together to sing *The Messiah*. As music has a broader appeal even than the theatre, it is not surprising that London became filled with concert halls by the middle of the century; in fact, it was probably better supplied than it is today. Furthermore, the fame of London audiences, both their willingness to pay and their capacity to understand, brought a stream of great European musicians to London – not only Handel, who stayed and became in a sense entirely English, but Haydn and Mozart and the younger Bachs. In the seventeenth century it had taken almost decades for the Italian music of Corelli to reach England, whereas by 1760 British audiences were already in touch with what was happening in Europe, whether in opera, concert or chamber music; and, indeed, London was the greatest centre of musical publishing. As with the theatre, the great expansion of music led to the promotion of star performers, many of them Italian: vocalists such as Noferi, or such instrumentalists as Lidarti; nor were all stars confined to fashionable musical circles.

Clearly, cheap instruments and cheap music, either for sale or for hire, made eighteenth-century England one of the leading musical nations of the western world – less rich in composers, certainly, than Italy, France or Germany, but freer by far from aristocratic or princely patronage: musicians of every kind could live and work more independently than anywhere else in Europe. And who else achieved the national fame of Handel?

Johann Zoffany *A Family Party – the Minuet*, 1780–83.

With such an explosion of musical activity, the ancillary arts – particularly dancing – acquired a greater sophistication and a more formal social organization. During the seventeenth century there were basically two types of dances: those of the court and the sophisticated houses of the aristocracy and gentry – the pavanes and galliards of the Italian Renaissance court – and the country dances around a maypole on a village green or in a farmer's barn, traditional dances, sometimes of a very local nature. These often became riotous and unseemly and the target of fierce puritanical denunciation. Although the gentry might, on occasion, go to and enjoy a country dance, the pavanes and galliards were not to be seen on the village green.

There were no balls or assemblies for which one purchased a ticket. One danced with friends or with one's neighbours. But from early in the eighteenth century, first at the spas and then in villages great and small, balls were organized on a subscription basis, usually in winter on the night of the full moon, to make travelling easier. These dances were held either in the splendid new assembly rooms which had become such a feature of provincial cultural life, or in a room at the inn especially designed for the purpose. Naturally, although country dances remained an essential part of the repertoire of every ball, complex group dances of a much more formal kind – the minuet for example – began to dominate the programme. These were regarded as more sophisticated and much more genteel. Such provincial assemblies varied greatly. The great race-week balls at York in the brilliant Egyptian rooms were a rendezvous for the northern aristocracy and gentry, whereas at the subscription dance at Harleston in Norfolk, held in a smallish room at the village inn, the company consisted of young farmers, their sisters and an occasional attorney or doctor. Nevertheless, a sense of fashionable delight was common to them both. Dances for which one paid an entrance fee also broadened the range of social contact, made for superior professional musical accomplishment, and because ambition was so strong, impelled people to take formal instruction from the fast-growing profession of dancing masters. So ardent were middle-class women to become adept in the latest fashionable steps that they became the prey of unscrupulous teachers and a butt of the satirists; but no one can deny that, as with so many aspects of eighteenth-century culture, the commercialization of dancing brought great opportunities for enjoyment to greater numbers of men and women.

What is true of literature, the theatre and music was equally true of the visual arts. Britain's contribution to Europe's artistic heritage, except perhaps for architecture, has been modest, but at least in the eighteenth and early nineteenth centuries, with painters such as Reynolds, Gainsborough, Constable and Turner, it made a significant contribution, whilst in the development of horse painting and sporting pictures it was unrivalled. Art often responds to affluence. The market in pictures, either in old masters or commissioned portraits and paintings, was small in the seventeenth century, but from 1700 onwards it steadily grew. By 1800 Britain was alive with painters, engravers, watercolourists, satirists and drawing masters; even provincial society, especially in East Anglia, possessed schools of painting of quite exceptional quality. Although portraits, including those of horses, dogs and prize cattle, held the field, there was a demand for landscapes, conversation pieces, genre studies and 'history pieces'. History pictures that enshrined contemporary events, such as *The Death of Wolfe at Quebec*, had an immense sale when engraved. Indeed, it was the vigour of British art that led to the foundation of the Royal Academy in 1768. This had been projected for many years; in fact, Vertue had discussed the project with George III's father. The Academy was established not only to give a mark of social as well as professional distinction to the leading painters and sculptors of the day, but also, by the yearly exhibitions, to set a seal of approbation on work being produced. Another of its purposes was to teach – to help produce yet more artists. William Hogarth, arguably Britain's most original artist, disliked artistic societies and exhibitions, and indeed put on a remarkable spoof exhibition of doctored inn-signs, so creating, as it were, an anti-academy. Hogarth feared that an academy, if established, would stifle originality, strengthen convention and create a body of self-flattering oligarchs. For many decades this did not happen, and the Academy did represent, if not always as soon as it might have done, the foremost painters and sculptors of Britain.

Perhaps the most remarkable feature of the surging British art market was the relatively minor role played by noble patronage, if one excludes portraiture. There was some: J.R.Cozens obtained support from the eccentric William Beckford of Fonthill; Turner was greatly helped by Lord Egremont at Petworth; but a surprising number of artists of the second and even third rank made an adequate living from the support of the public alone. Artists such as Mary Moser or the Morlands, or even stranger painters, such as Fuseli, made a very tolerable living. Of course, there was an occasional artist of great talent, such as Richard Wilson, who was forced to live close to poverty. But many portraitists and landscape painters made considerable fortunes, not only the Reynoldses, Gainsboroughs and Constables, but also painters such as George Lambert, George Stubbs and even provincial artists like Joseph Wright of Derby. The country was swept with a passion for art, which meant that young artists, minor artists, or any artists with energy could add to their economic buoyancy through teaching.

Academies, especially the very famous one run by Sir James Thornhill in St Martin's Lane, had existed for the teaching of art in the early eighteenth century, but such academies were few and confined to London. Neither in London nor in the provinces were artist-instructors easily come by at that time, nor were there many drawing masters of ability, just as there were, of course, very, very few books of instruction, and none manufactured for a mass market.

Skill in drawing was useful for many commercial activities: textiles and pottery are two obvious manufactures that needed trained commercial artists. In addition, the capacity to paint a watercolour became a mark of gentility, particularly for girls, so that artists' materials and the teaching of art mushroomed in the mid-eighteenth century. Joseph Wright's *An Academy by Lamplight* (p.38) or Paul Sandby's *A Lady Seated at a Drawing Board* (p. 36) express vividly different aspects of this remarkable expansion in the teaching of art. Perhaps the vast interest in drawing and watercolours is nowhere better illustrated than in the series of admirable handbooks, many of them of great beauty in their own right, which taught landscape, portrait, and particularly flower painting, or gave instruction in the art of perspective and the use of colour. Naturally, this phenomenon had many other repercussions. Interest in the work of British artists was high, and exhibitions of their work drew huge crowds; indeed, not only was The Society for the Encouragement of the Arts once forced to charge an entrance fee because of the disreputable mob that poured in, but the proprietors of Vauxhall and Ranelagh Gardens allowed artists to hang their canvases there to attract visitors.

It was a world made for the dilettante and the collector. All young aristocrats who had made the Grand Tour had been exposed to the

Paul Sandby *A Lady Seated at a Drawing Board*, c. 1760.

artistic delights of Italy, and few came back without works of art. To be an amateur of painting was the sign of a gentleman, and the painted canvases, leather hangings and old Mortlake tapestries of the English country houses were steadily removed and replaced by fashionable masters, old and new. The Bologna school had its day, as did the Venetian; indeed, Canaletto spent several years in London. By the middle of the eighteenth century the greatest market for Italian art was probably England, and seventeenth-century Dutch and Flemish artists were almost as popular. The French, the Spanish, and above all the Germans lagged behind. But great 'gentlemen's collections' were formed, one of many examples being that at Thirlestaine House.

Lower-middle-class men and women, however, could not afford old masters, neither could they afford the relatively cheap new masters – the Dances, the Mortimers, the Morlands and the rest – yet they wished to adorn the walls of their houses with art. And the response to this demand was a growth in prints, so that engravings of all kinds flourished to a degree never before known in England.

In many ways Hogarth was as responsible as any artist for developing the growth of the print trade and making it worth an artist's while to make prints. Hogarth's fury at seeing his *Harlot's Progress* pirated by other print dealers led him to secure, in 1737, the Copyright Act, by which the artist kept the rights of his own print for ten years. His copyright secured, Hogarth exploited every public occasion to make prints and sell them. His engraving of Lord Lovat, the Jacobite peer who was beheaded in 1746, sold 10,000 copies and made him £300. Richard Wilson, desperate for money, sold the rights of his *Niobe* to Woollett, the print dealer, who netted £2,000 from its sale. Old masters did not sell so well as contemporary prints – those of Lovat or Wilkes, for example – but they sold well. In fact, remarkable collections of superlative prints, made for the discriminating collector rather than the public at large, were produced by Boydell and Bartolozzi; indeed, Boydell was so fascinated with the print and so extravagant in the planning of his Shakespeare Gallery that he was finally brought to bankruptcy and ruin. Nevertheless, those who kept their eye firmly on the mass market made fortunes. By 1800 no town of any size was without its print shop; most booksellers ran prints as a sideline; and there were even libraries where prints could be borrowed.

Yet it is doubtful whether old or new master paintings, or even the contemporary history prints of Hogarth, could have sustained so huge a trade. There is no doubt that much of the burgeoning of the

Joseph Wright of Derby *An Academy by Lamplight*, c. 1768–69.

print market was due to the development of the satirical print. The freedom of English life, the lack of any form of literary censorship, opened up a field of social and political satire that was quite unique in eighteenth-century Europe. These prints were often vulgar, sometimes obscene, occasionally erotic, and at times pornographic, but always biting in their comment on social customs or political events. And the medium was brilliantly exploited by Gilray, Bunbury, Rowlandson, Cruikshank and a host of lesser artists.

In sum, art had achieved a mass market: museums and galleries were established; the practice of art, both professional and amateur, was widespread; and, through the print trade, art could reach the poorest tavern, the humblest home.

Then art pushed well beyond its own boundaries and became the handmaid of commerce, industry and even science. It is odd how the traditional representation of birds, animals, fishes and flowers had continued generation after generation. Albrecht Dürer's highly fanciful representation of the rhinoceros had been followed for generations after his death – the same falsities depicted time and time again. The discoveries of sixteenth- and seventeenth-century scientists had, more often than not, remained the arcane knowledge of an élite. Popular science, combined with a new interest in mechanical devices, began only in the eighteenth century. Lectures which demonstrated electrical apparatuses became extremely popular, but even they never secured the audiences achieved by the 'Great Orrery', an instrument for giving the position of the planets in the solar system, which travelled the length and breadth of the land, instructing young as well as old in the new world of scientific marvels. Joseph Wright captures the same spirit in his painting *The Air Pump*. Never before had inventors and technicians become famous public figures so quickly, and the portraits of the great figures of the industrial revolution – Sir Richard Arkwright, James Brindley, Josiah Wedgwood, John Wilkinson and many others – were soon filling the print shops.

The new popular science added an air of excitement to a world that seemed ever-expanding, in which new avenues of intellectual inquiry were opening. Curiosity about the natural world, about distant regions, had always been strong, but limited to a small cultured élite. These confines were now broken, and ordinary men and women flocked to the museums and menageries that sprang up not only in London but elsewhere. Sir Ashton Lever's Museum in Leicester Square and Wallis's Museum drew large audiences for years. Many pleasure gardens established aviaries of exotic birds and occasionally set up a monkey house. Circuses possessed their lion tamers and their elephants. By the early nineteenth century the London Zoo was the Mecca of young and old. Such establishments whetted the appetite for knowledge and, even more importantly, engendered a sense of multiple worlds, of limitless horizons of strange and exotic lands stretching beyond the confines of Europe. Obviously, the widening interest in the natural world drew to it men of strong scientific bent. Through Linnaeus and also Buffon, the drive to systematize and bring order into the chaos of nature was very powerful. As birds, animals and flowers were studied with precision, art joined forces with science. George Edwards's beautiful volumes of British birds was a milestone in the history of exact ornithology. Flower studies too – witness the great volumes of *The London Flora* – became more precise, more scientific, if no less ravishing to the eye. So passionate an interest in the living world, plus, it must be admitted, a keen eye to profit, led to experimentation. Bakewell of Leicestershire was the most famous of animal breeders, but there were many others trying to achieve the heaviest ox, the fleeciest sheep. And throughout the land there was a vast array of florists breeding carnations and auriculas for their yearly competitions, in which prizes were given for new and spectacular hybrids. The experimental attitude was no longer confined to the gentlemen of the Royal Society; it had spread like a dye through society itself. And immense strides forward were made. Knowledge of the anatomy of animals became more detailed and more exact: one only needs to compare the works of Snape and Stubbs on the anatomy of the horse to realize the difference a few decades made to all fields of natural history. From racing pigeons to cucumbers, men were dissecting, peering through their microscopes, drawing what they saw with exemplary accuracy, and experimenting through inbreeding or crossbreeding. They bred the racehorse that we know today. But what must be stressed is that this preoccupation with breeding – whether it meant finding sweeter singing strains of canaries, more vividly striped carnations, auriculas of a deeper blue or horses that were fleet over a mile or powerful for twenty – reached deep into society. To experiment with living things was no longer a fearful meddling with God's Creation, but a commonplace activity.

And it was natural in the eighteenth century that this preoccupation with breeding should be involved with man's sporting activities, for they were closely involved with animals, whether racing them, hunting them or pitting one against another. The horse, as I have said, preoccupied eighteenth-century society: its motor power was essential and its beauty captivated; the essence of the horse was strength and speed. Gentlemen and farmers, proud of the qualities of the horses they owned, had wagered with their neighbours for centuries. The gentlemen of the court and the gentry in the country – owners of strings of horses – had begun in the late sixteenth and early seventeenth centuries to adopt one or two very favourable spots for racing horses – Newmarket Heath in the east, Doncaster and York in the north and Epsom and Ascot near London. They would meet there and spend a few days, or even a week or two, racing. Another great racing occasion was assize-week. This brought the gentry into the chief town of the shire – Exeter, Chester, Derby and the like – and, bent on mixing pleasure with business, they would race their horses for personal wagers. Towards the end of the seventeenth century, as with so many aspects of English cultural life, this amateur, quasi-haphazard process began to change. Charles II loved Newmarket, and during his reign it became the centre of horse-racing and the home of its growing professionalism.

Between 1680 and 1730 there was an explosion of race-meetings, which proliferated everywhere to such a degree that parliament had to check their growth. There was also a danger of utmost confusion, for rules tended to be local and were often agreed to just before a race. Gradually 'the judgment of Newmarket' became accepted as the arbiter of racing rules; and by the 1750s the Jockey Club there was in control. By then the sport had become systematized. The Racing Calendar, started in 1727, listed all races and their exact length, previous years' winners and the nature of the going. A number of races – for Gold Cups (or, in Scotland, sometimes gold teapots) – had acquired a star rating and brought together owners from varied regions. The professional trainer, first established for royal horses by William III, had become generally established by mid-century; professional jockeys had almost entirely eliminated the amateur rider by 1750; and racecourses themselves had been greatly improved. Many of them had permanent grandstands, where the more affluent racegoers could avoid the crowds that swarmed to watch and bet and generally riot. Enclosures for the élite soon followed. On course betting, which previously had been face-to-face, was also systematized by Tattersalls towards the end of the century. Indeed, by then, racing was a complex industry of breeders, trainers, jockeys and owners, which involved very large capital sums and drew tens of thousands of onlookers every year. The great classic races, the St Leger, the Oaks and the Derby, actually became national events. The Derby was all London's festival, as indeed was Ascot. Thomas Rowlandson's *Racing at Newmarket* (p. 115) illustrated the public image of racing. The private sport of kings had become a mass entertainment. Intense competition, steep betting and valuable prizes naturally affected the sport. It led to endless chicanery which demanded stronger and stronger rules. But competition also led to publicity: great races such as the Derby and the Oaks were puffed in the press to create public interest – almost in fact a public obsession. Jockeys and horses were used in a similar way to heighten public interest. The first stallions to capture the public imagination were the great Arabians – Lord Godolphin's, Mr Byerley's and Mr Darby's; they dominated the race tracks of their day, their victories or defeats discussed throughout the land. By the middle of the century horses of quite exceptional quality, combining great speed with stamina, were being bred – horses whose blood, however diluted, still runs through the pedigree horses of today. The most famous – Flying Childers, Lustre and Eclipse – became stars in their own right, particularly Eclipse whose portrait filled the prints and whose name graced many taverns. He was never beaten in any race, and he was the first stallion to net a fortune by standing at stud for his owner, O'Kelley, an Irish adventurer. Jockeys, too, cultivated publicity.

They and the trainers who hired them knew its value, not only because it enabled them to put up their own fees, but also because it personalized the races and drew in the crowds. Jockeys like Scott and Oakley were as famous as Eclipse or Flying Childers. And again, owners could not avoid publicity. Lord George Bentinck, the first man to use a horse-box, was glamourized in the press and in prints, while he and his friends cast a glow of aristocratic glamour over the sport with their huge bets and blatant life-styles. So avid was public interest that, in the early nineteenth century, racing bred the first sporting journalist, and one of incomparable ability, Pierce Egan, who wrote about 'The Fancy' – the cant name for owners, trainers, jockeys and hangers-on, who were addicted not only to the turf but also very often to boxing, which, by the 1800s, had become as much of an industry as racing.

Boxing became professionalized during the century, developing through John Broughton – a fine boxer but an even finer entrepreneur – a strict code of rules. As publicity increased, so did the audiences, and all England Championships drew vast crowds: the great Mendoza-Humphrey's fight was deliberately staged in the middle of England so that the audience could be nationwide. And Mendoza's victory promoted him to the stardom we associate with

George Stubbs *Eclipse*, 1770.

Mohammed Ali: there were Mendoza mugs, Mendoza statuettes, Mendoza handkerchiefs, Mendoza autographs, Mendoza exhibitions and Mendoza memoirs – indeed, a Mendoza industry. Pugilism, however, was very nearly outlawed, for men and women began to turn sharply against brutality in sport: bearbaiting was stopped; so was bull-running; and one of the most popular of all sports, cockfighting, was, after a long struggle, finally suppressed. What was encouraged were games of skill. Philidor, the great chess-master, helped to make chess a popular game; similarly, billiards ceased to be an aristocratic game and became the sport of the middle classes; educational games – jigsaw puzzles and games similar to scrabble or monopoly – became all the rage; and the lower classes were encouraged to take up pigeon racing or to course their greyhounds. Blood sports that were fostered were those which exterminated vermin or produced food. These were thought to be part of Nature's great and rational design. Here, at least, the benefits outweighed the pain and brutality.

Eighteenth-century society enjoyed – indeed lived much more than we do – out of doors. They adored the countryside. They loved their pleasure gardens. Thus rural sports – so long as they were not directly sadistic – continued to flourish, particularly those of a gentle nature, such as bowls, or those thought to be manly, such as fencing, or rural sports that were as traditional as the roast beef of England, such as hawking or archery. As with horse-racing and boxing, some traditional sports – cricket, rowing matches and yacht racing – became systematized in their rules and organized for spectator participation. But much outdoor sport remained personal and private. Fishing or angling enjoyed a quite exceptional boom. Rivers and lakes were deliberately stocked with fish, and angling parties were very fashionable – the aristocrats performing very grandly in their barges, the lower-middle class tramping on foot with rod and line. As a result, London and the provinces now had many shops that specialized entirely in fishing gear, and they thrived.

The greatest of all rural sports, however, were hunting and shooting. The improvements in the sporting gun in the late seventeenth and early eighteenth centuries had enabled the sportsman to shoot birds on the wing, though the guns were not exceptionally accurate, for variation was considerable and great skill was needed. So addicted did the gentry become to shooting that savage laws protecting their rights over game littered the statute book, but poaching, of course, remained endemic. A state of submerged strife between gentry and peasants over game went on

John Wootton *Preparing for the Hunt*, c. 1720–40.

until modern times and still persists. But pheasants, partridges, stags, and, amongst fish, salmon and trout, tended to be preserved by and for the upper classes. To own a shoot or fishing rights in a river argued social status.

And the same became true of fox-hunting. In the early eighteenth century fox-hunting was ill-regulated and ill-organized, largely the sport of farmers; only the stag had true cachet. Nevertheless, deer forests were getting smaller, stags were rare, and foxes were not only common but gave magnificent sport. This, too, was made more exciting by the practice of enclosure, the breaking up of the great open fields into small compact units surrounded by small thorn hedges, which created greater obstacles for the huntsmen and added danger to the sport. The most highly enclosed parts of England were the Midlands, particularly Leicestershire and Northamptonshire, yet at the same time this country had low, rolling hills which made for wide vistas, so it was ideal fox-hunting country. The great hunts began to form – the Quorn, the Belvoir, the Cottesmore and the Pytchley. The rules were formalized, the counties divided up, the subscriptions rose, the sport became the rage of the gentry and, as with racing or the theatre, turned up its mythic figures, Squire Osbaldeston or John Mytton.

Hunting and shooting, angling parties and hawking were the active parts of social life in the country. Although the English upper classes were much more urban than they had been, drawn now to London for the season, nevertheless they were still deeply rooted in the countryside and were, for generations to come, to remain so. Even if they lived a great deal of the year in London, with its endless rounds of theatre, concerts, balls and gaming tables, they lavished money on their country estates, rebuilding, redecorating their houses, constantly embellishing their parks and gardens, and from time to time filling their houses to overflowing with friends and their servants. Often Sir Robert Walpole had fifty or sixty guests at one of the famous Houghton Congresses, at which not only were hundreds of pounds spent on candles to make the house blaze, but the food was gargantuan and the drink stupendous. By day they hunted, by night they feasted, and at all times intrigued. Wootton's splendiferous picture *Preparing For the Hunt* (opposite) gives a vivid idea of the sumptuous quality of English country-house life.

The heart of their rural world was the country house, but like a splendid jewel, it required an elaborate setting. Indeed, the setting became as important, at times more important, than the house itself, and often more expensive. In the sixteenth and early seventeenth centuries, gentlemen had created elaborate formal gardens that were more expensive to maintain than to create, although some of the great parterres, such as Queen Anne's at Hampton Court or, on a less elaborate scale, Mr Pierrepont's, which looked to Versailles and Le Notre, could, and did, eat up money. However, formal gardens vanished and were replaced by a 'natural landscape'. This was natural only in the sense that nature was not regimented, but it was certainly improved. Capability Brown and, afterwards, Humphry Repton thought nothing of razing hills, planting woods or creating lakes. They took the same liberties with landscape as did a landscape painter – moving a hill, setting up a temple or a folly to give a focal point to the vista. Serpentine walks threaded the woods and bordered the lakes. Grecian urns, statues, obelisks, artificial waterfalls, sometimes a Chinese pagoda, or even a live hermit in a grotto, brought a touch of whimsy or urbanity to a landscape that looked so natural, yet was so completely man-made. Viewing these elaborate gardens became a summer sport of the upper and middle classes, who were as knowledgeable as professionals on the merits of vistas. Some gardens, such as Lord Cobham's at Stowe, became so fashionable that entrance fees were charged, elaborate guidebooks as well as prints for mementoes were sold, and teas were provided for the weary. The amount of capital involved in these vast gardens was very large. The removal of a hill or the planting of five or six woods was nothing untoward, even for a gentleman of only moderate affluence. Planting became the rage, but it demanded tens of thousands of trees, not merely seedlings, for no-one planting seedlings could hope to see what he designed. Hence the wood had to be planted with three- or four-year-old, nursery-grown trees, and was usually surrounded by expensive ten- or twelve-year-old trees so that the desired effect could be achieved with reasonable rapidity. This demand stimulated nurseries, and elaborate catalogues containing hundreds of items were produced by such famous nurserymen as the Perfects of Pontefract. They could provide not only tens of thousands of nursery-grown beech trees, elms, oaks or firs, but also many exotics which they deliberately boosted in order to extend their markets. They and other seedsmen created a fashion for camellias from Japan and veronicas from the Falkland Islands. Indeed, most of the great landscape gardens contained trees and shrubs that were totally alien to Britain. Nor were the pleasures of gardening confined to the gentry; many small market towns had a club, usually called the Sons of Flora, which organized competitions for the best carnations and auriculas, sometimes giving special prizes for new hybrids, and whose members might trade rare varieties for a guinea a time. There was a rage for flowers. They festooned ladies' dresses and hats; they were painted on their furniture, lacquered on their trays, carved into their chimney pieces and fired on to their china. Covent Garden market blazed with the colours of flowers as well as vegetables. And naturally enough, artists painted them – the professionals occasionally, the amateurs constantly.

Although money was poured into gardens, with their shrubs and flowers, and into exotic fruits in heated greenhouses – pineapples, melons, nectarines and the like – the house was not neglected. Not only must its architecture and its setting impress, but so must its contents, and the critical eye of the country-house visitor was not confined to pictures and statuary.

The furniture might be elaborate, including splendid pagoda-like looking-glasses, all gilt and glitter, with chinamen perched in improbable places; it might be japanned in brilliant vermillion or creamy white, as well as the more commonplace black and green; or it might be elaborately inlaid in French style or beautifully carved.

The chimney pieces were of the finest marble, and festooned with vases in blue-john and ormolu, with the urns of Josiah Wedgwood or the figures of Bow and Chelsea. And yet the enjoyment of these rich furnishings was not confined to an aristocratic class; there was a growing middle-class market, too, for simpler and cheaper furnishings made in the same style, a market that Hepplewhite and Sheraton exploited in furniture and Wedgwood in china, not to mention Matthew Boulton and others, who provided the middle classes with the elaborate candelabra and dishes in silver plate that at first sight looked no different from the aristocracy's silver. As with music, painting and literature, the decorative arts escaped from the confines of a rich élite and reached a mass market, a fact which would have struck anyone strolling about London in the 1770s, when retail shops proliferated. One of the simpler pleasures of life, yet one never enjoyed by the mass of mankind, and one which for thousands in eighteenth-century England was a novelty, is the walk down a shopping street with money in the pocket to spend – sauntering from shop to shop, hesitating, comparing and finally taking the plunge. As shoppers increased, shopkeepers tried to entice them within. They invented the bow window, which put more on display; they invented show-cases and elaborate self-puffing trade cards; and the ingenious Mr Wedgwood set out dining tables complete with his latest choice services displayed on the best table linen and accompanied by his friend Boulton's cutlery and candelabra.

Since fashion entices guineas from the pocket quicker than any shopkeeper's art of display, it was increasingly exploited: textile patterns began to change every year; hats varied suddenly from the simplicity of a maid-servant's flower-bedecked straw to elaborate concoctions that dazzled the imagination – huge cornucopias of fruit, a Covent Garden of flower bouquets, sometimes even cages with birds! And hair styles for women and for men changed as rapidly as hats, sometimes reaching such extravagant, farcical heights that it became impossible for a woman of fashion to sit in a sedan chair without putting her head out of the window!

Like music or the visual arts – indeed, like the country houses and their cultured landscapes – fashions need an audience. All were made for delight, for show, to display what the eighteenth century called *ton*; and where better than at a party, whether a dinner party, a card party, a private ball or merely a picnic? As in all affluent societies, men and women pursued food and drink remorselessly, creating their own snobbery of fine dishes, exotic fruits and rare wines. It is not surprising that vintage wines first came into vogue in the eighteenth century, or that great chefs achieved the same star rating as Eclipse or Garrick; indeed, Carème, the Prince Regent's chef, was a national figure whose creations were the talk of the fashionable world. Of course, as with hats and hair styles, parties were carried to excess. The Prince Regent and most of the rich consumed and wasted gargantuan quantities of meat and fish, fruit and vegetables, and wines of every hue. And again, not only the rich ate well or to excess. Food was, except in times of war, reasonably cheap, and, as with more refined pursuits, the delight in eating pushed deeper into the population. Eighteenth-century men and women liked a feast and constantly discovered reasons for holding one. After all, for the lower-middle classes an abundance of food was as much a novelty as cheap prints on their walls or a hired harpsichord in their parlour. And yet it must be stressed that these people were still a minority, and a small one. Probably more than half of the population still lived meanly, possessing little, toiling hard, often hungry. The gates to happiness had been opened, but only narrowly; they were not wide open for all and sundry, yet they could not, in Britain, be closed again. Slowly and inexorably they would be pushed open wider and wider, allowing the millions, for the first time in human history, to enjoy some of the civilities, the culture, the arts – indeed, the leisured happiness – which hitherto had been the perquisite of a narrow and highly aristocratic élite.

# PART TWO

*The Portfolios*

The prefaces to the portfolios deal, on occasion, with subjects covered in more detail in the text of Part I but their intention is to help immediate understanding of the pictures without searching the text.

# *Home Life*

Only recently have historians begun to realize how austere, almost bleak, family life was before the eighteenth century – not, of course, for all families; in all ages there have been warm, affectionate, spontaneous men and women with ebullient and loving natures. Most people, however, respond to the social attitudes of their age, no matter how odd or severe. The seventeenth century – in the New World as well as the Old – was, as far as the household was concerned, a cold time. Children were harshly disciplined, wives rarely companions, demonstrations of affection rare. Nor were the amenities and comforts of life numerous.

In the eighteenth century there was a notable change. Art betrays the difference: the conversation pieces and the family portraits, where parents and children are shown travelling, fishing, playing or learning together, speak of a new intimacy, a new style of domestic happiness. Children's books, children's toys, the availability of games and amusements which instructed the child, from miniature microscopes to tiny printing presses, all indicate a growing involvement by parents in a child's happiness and education.

The home itself became an object of greater interest and larger expenditure. Not only the aristocracy, but also the middle classes spent far more money than ever before on furnishings and on domestic delights. The decorative arts produced men of exceptional talent – Kent, Vile, Chippendale and Sheraton, Hepplewhite and many others, whose patterns were copied by skilled craftsmen throughout the country. The more elaborate productions of Kent, Vile and Chippendale were extremely expensive, usually designed for the magnificence of a noble house or regal setting, but the mass of Georgian furniture – so keenly sought today – was of a simple, natural elegance. In other decorative arts there is the same combination of highly ornate, expensive pieces for the aristocracy and mass-produced elegance for the middle classes; for example, Josiah Wedgwood manufactured elaborate vases, copied from antiques recently discovered at Pompeii, in small numbers for very high prices to decorate the mantelpieces of the wealthy; at the same time he made tens of thousands of dinner and tea services – charming, simple, not cheap, but within the means of the middle classes.



And there can be no doubt that the passion to possess things grew in eighteenth-century England. One of the greatest delights of leisure for many men and women is shopping. The bow window designed to entice people within the shop was an eighteenth-century invention; the dining table laid out with glass, china and silverware was another; yearly changes in textile fashions a third. In consequence the home grew more comfortable, more beautiful, more of a haven for family happiness, a private world in which men and women could exercise their taste for their personal delight.

As with decorative arts, so with food and drink. In the 1730s a popular song – 'The Roast Beef of Old England' – swept the land; meat was indeed consumed in astonishing quantities, but more remarkable still was the increase in varieties of fruit and vegetables. Although there was a great deal of hunger and deprivation amongst the all too numerous poor, never before had so many Englishmen eaten or drunk so much; food was bountiful and never before had so much port and claret been imported into England or so much beer brewed. Although most English people were very high minded, full of moral purpose in their pursuit of happiness, they did not forget the simpler carnal delights.

Arthur Devis *A Family Group in a Garden.*

LEFT, ABOVE William Hogarth *The Graham Children*, 1742.

LEFT Philip Reinagle *Mrs Congreve and Family*, 1782.

ABOVE Engraving by George Cruikshank *'At Home' in the Nursery, or The Masters and Misses Twoshoes Christmas Party*, 1826.

LEFT, ABOVE Charles Philips *Tea Party at Lord Harrington's House*, 1739.

LEFT Arthur Devis *Mr and Mrs William Atherton*, c. 1730–40.

ABOVE Sir Joshua Reynolds *The Ladies Waldegrave*, c. 1780.

TOP Design by Robert Adam for a wall of the music room of Home House, London.

ABOVE Ackermann print of the Wedgwood showrooms in St James's Square, London, 1809.

RIGHT Design for a secretary and bookcase from Thomas Sheraton's *Cabinet Maker and Upholsterer's Drawing Book*, 1791.

BELOW Trade card advertising James Wheeley's London wallpaper warehouse.

ABOVE Attrib. R. Collins *A Family at Tea*, c. 1730.

BELOW Thomas Rowlandson *The Glutton*, 1818.

ɔVE Great Kitchen at The Royal Pavilion, Brighton, designed by John Nash for the Prince Regent.

BELOW Print by M. Dubourg after James Pollard *Fruit Stall*, c. 1880.

# *Gardens*

Nature was considered to be the greatest handiwork of God. It stirred men's emotions, lifted their thoughts, soothed their spirits, bred a sense of awe: indeed, it entangled them in a world of feeling. Hence the best gardens were those which copied nature, or brought natural beauties into harmony. Addison and Pope both derided the old-fashioned English gardens with their topiary, emblematic flower beds of geometric complexity and gravelled walks. They were a deformity of nature, not an expression of its poetry.

William Kent, Charles Bridgman and 'Capability' Brown quickly uprooted the old gardens and replaced them with gardens which brought a 'natural' landscape almost into the house. True, they moved hills, created lakes, planted woods and made serpentine walks with carefully contrived vistas; they groomed and disciplined nature. Later in the century, the devotees of the picturesque thought they had groomed and disciplined it far too much. Like a landscape painter they deliberately designed a harmonious picture, and one that never lacked dramatic effects. Here and there they created an ivy-covered ruin, or a classical Temple to the Muses, built an obelisk or even, as at Kew, a Chinese pagoda to underline a point of perspective, or so that men and women might rest, give thought to the eternal verities, take tea amidst the delights of nature, or flirt more discreetly. But gardens were for happiness, that deeply valued eighteenth-century happiness which was based on an appreciation of the moral values. Landscapes, and therefore gardens, spoke the language of God – so, from Pope to Wordsworth, the poets wrote. Viewing these extraordinary gardens, such as Stourhead, or Lord Bathurst's at Cirencester, became a popular pastime, drawing hundreds of visitors every summer.

For most men and women, however, gardens were sheer delight in themselves, an expression of their own natures and their own predelictions. New varieties of trees, shrubs and flowers, as well as vegetables and fruit, were pouring into the country – hundreds of new species and varieties not only from the New World, but also from China and Japan. Camellias, rhododendrons, azaleas and magnolias, and many other species began to change the appearance of the English garden.



For those who could not afford a landscaped park, there were books which taught them how to create a suburban garden, and even manuals for the city merchant so that he might decorate his house with window boxes and tubs. Fascination with flowers was widespread; clubs of gardeners, the Sons of Flora, were to be found throughout the land, arranging competitions for flowers and fruit, exchanging rare plants and hybrids, creating that passion for gardening amongst all classes which has steadily grown over the last two centuries. A new industry of seedsmen and horticulturists flourished; the middle classes, as well as the aristocracy, could surround their houses with the beauties of nature. Another widespread delight was added to the happiness of man.

Trade card of nurseryman Henry Scott,
advertising, in particular, pineapples for sale.

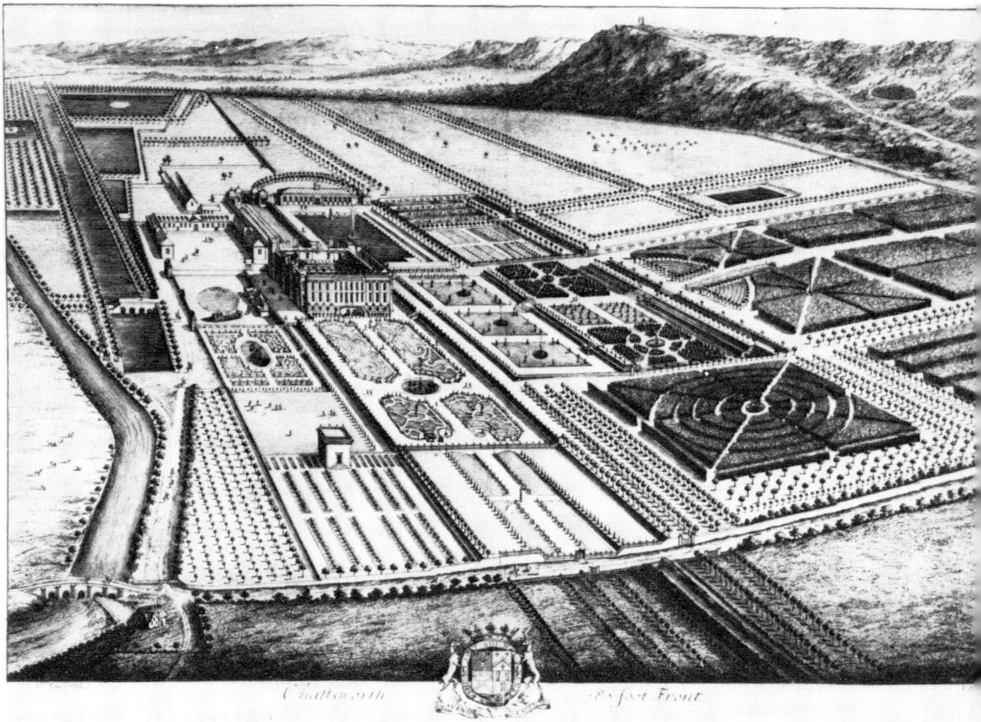
Chattsworth
foot Front

LEFT, ABOVE Engraving by L. Knyff *Chatsworth Garden, Derbyshire.*

LEFT Francis Nicholson *The Pantheon and Gothic Cottage at Stourhead*, 1813–14.

ABOVE Thomas Gainsborough *Gainsborough and his Wife (Conversation in a Park)*, c. 1746.

ABOVE Aquatint *The Chinese Pagoda and Bridge in St James's Park*, 1814.

LEFT The River God in a grotto at Stourhead, Wiltshire.

Paul Sandby *Deputy Ranger's Lodge, Windsor Great Park*, 1798.

OBSERVATIONS

ON

THE THEORY AND PRACTICE

OF

**Landscape Gardening.**

INCLUDING

SOME REMARKS

ON

GRECIAN AND GOTHIC ARCHITECTURE,

COLLECTED FROM

VARIOUS MANUSCRIPTS,

IN THE POSSESSION OF

THE DIFFERENT NOBLEMEN AND GENTLEMEN,

FOR WHOSE USE THEY WERE ORIGINALLY WRITTEN;

*THE WHOLE TENDING TO ESTABLISH FIXED PRINCIPLES IN THE RESPECTIVE ARTS.*

---

By H. REPTON, Esq.

---

LONDON:

*PRINTED BY T. BENSLEY, BOLT COURT,*

FOR J. TAYLOR, AT THE ARCHITECTURAL LIBRARY, HIGH HOLBORN.

1803.

LEFT, ABOVE James Lambert *A Garden at Lewes*, 1787.

LEFT Title page of Humphry Repton's *Observations on the Theory and Practice of Landscape Gardening*, 1803.

ABOVE Thomas Rowlandson *The Gardener's Offering*.

# *Literature*

The eighteenth century witnessed an unprecedented spread of literature. In the seventeenth century publishers had concentrated mainly on divinity and the classics, and to a lesser extent on histories and natural philosophy. Plays, poetry and romances played a small part in the bookseller's world. Most books were large – folios and quartos dominated the publishers' lists, and they were expensive. By 1800 all had changed. The size of books was smaller, the range of prices was greater, and there was much more specialization. One of the most fundamental changes was the growth in female readership, a readership assiduously cultivated by the increasing tribe of novelists, good, bad and indifferent. But every type of readership was catered for – children, gardeners, cooks, musicians, artists, lawyers, doctors, numismatists, bird-fanciers, travel addicts. For bibliophiles there were very expensive, beautifully illustrated books that have rarely, if ever, been surpassed. And booksellers pushed their wares in new and novel ways. They started circulating libraries, held book auctions, published expensive books in parts to secure a wider readership and developed the second-hand catalogue. They also took shares in publications that were too costly for one publisher, and made certain of their profits by opening subscription lists before the book was published, sometimes even before the book was written.

For the first time it was possible for a quite considerable body of writers, women as well as men, to eke out a living by their pens, and a few made enough to live handsomely. Alexander Pope, Samuel Johnson, Oliver Goldsmith and many others acquired social distinction as well as profit from their writing.

Amateur as well as professional writers had far more outlets for their creative talents. Magazines, mostly modelled on *The Spectator*, which had had a huge success in Queen Anne's reign, grew in number, and they were always hungry for material. In consequence never has so much bad poetry been published as in the eighteenth century, when it seems that almost anyone who could write tried his or her hand at verse. So magazines – *The Gentleman's*, *The London* and *The Ladies'* – kept a devoted readership for decade after decade, thriving on a mixture of hard fact, morally uplifting essays and execrable verse.



Nor was this spread of literature restricted to the middle classes:

cheap books were available for a penny or less; do-it-yourself books could be bought for sixpence; and so could simple primers on all academic subjects. And bookshops abounded in cheap ballads and old fairy stories. No small town lacked a bookseller, who was often a printer too. To possess a library was a mark of gentility, but books also found their way into the humblest cottage. Conservatives worried about the spread of literacy, radicals gloried in it, but most Englishmen and women were oblivious to any consequences, and read for the delight which it brought them. Their imaginations were provoked, their knowledge increased, their horizons broadened and their appetites for life whetted. Reading brought happiness and encouraged people to pursue it.

Thomas Rowlandson *A Book Auction*, c. 1805–15.

WILLIAMS'S LIBRARY, CHELTENHAM.

HALL'S LIBRARY AT MARGATE.

LEFT, ABOVE Trade card advertising Williams's Library, Cheltenham.

LEFT Aquatint after Georgiana Keate *Hall's Library at Margate*, 1789.

TOP Isaac Cruikshank *The Circulating Library*, c. 1800–05.

ABOVE Design for a library table from Thomas Sheraton's *Cabinet Maker and Upholsterer's Drawing Book*, 1791.

ABOVE Sir Joshua Reynolds *Joseph Baretti*; the sitter is seen scrutinising the print of a pocket-size book.

RIGHT Mezzotint after Henry Morland *Reading by a Paper-bell Shade*, c. 1769.

Morland pinx.t — Published as the Act directs — Phil. Dawe fecit

*Reading by a Paper-bell Shade.*

Printed for Carington Bowles, Map & Printseller, at No. 69 in St. Pauls Church Yard, London.

THE

# LIFE

AND

STRANGE SURPRIZING

## ADVENTURES

OF

*ROBINSON CRUSOE,*

Of *YORK*, MARINER:

Who lived Eight and Twenty Years, all alone in an un-inhabited Island on the Coast of AMERICA, near the Mouth of the Great River of OROONOQUE;

Having been cast on Shore by Shipwreck, where-in all the Men perished but himself.

WITH

An Account how he was at last as strangely deliver'd by PYRATES.

*Written by Himself.*

*LONDON;*

Printed for W. TAYLOR at the *Ship* in *Pater-Noster-Row.* MDCCXIX. 1766

THE

# HISTORY

OF

*TOM JONES,*

A

## FOUNDLING.

In SIX VOLUMES.

By HENRY FIELDING, Esq;

—*Mores hominum multorum vidit.*—

*LONDON:*

Printed for A. MILLAR, over-against *Catharine-street* in the *Strand.*

MDCCXLIX.

FAR LEFT, ABOVE Joseph Wright of Derby *Brooke Boothby*, 1781.

FAR LEFT Portrait of Jane Austen by her sister Cassandra, 1810.

ABOVE Frontispiece and title page of the first edition of Daniel Defoe's *Robinson Crusoe*, 1719.

LEFT Title page of the first edition of Henry Fielding's *Tom Jones*, 1749.

# *Theatre*

The Civil War, followed by the Commonwealth which banned all play acting as the work of the devil, dealt a terrible blow at the brilliant theatrical development that had begun in the reign of Queen Elizabeth. Recovery in Charles II's reign, in spite of his own interest, was slow. Theatres in London were few, often ill attended, good new plays rare, and, as with the comedies of Congreve and Wycherley, written for a social élite. In the provinces actors used a barn, hired a room in an inn, or, with luck, obtained permission from the town officials to use the guildhall, but there were no theatres in the provinces built for acting.

As with literature, the theatre blossomed in the eighteenth century; long before 1800 every market town, however small, had its own, specially built theatre, often tiny but always elegant. They were visited by London actors in the summer, or by troupes from the big towns nearby, and often provided a theatre for amateurs, especially schoolboys. Grammar Schools often put on plays at Christmas – usually for charity. In London, theatres became very large – by 1794 Drury Lane could accommodate over three and a half thousand spectators. Maybe the London theatres were too large, for the London play-going audience was not vast, hence plays rarely ran for very long and there was a constant demand for new plays. Over two thousand were produced between 1750 and 1800, most of them tedious, heavy with sentimentality, middle-class morality and the work ethic. Only Goldsmith and Sheridan have survived. But the acting was magnificent – and with David Garrick the star system triumphed; his name was sufficient to pack the theatre. And there was far greater variety of theatrical entertainment in London than there had ever been before. Pantomime started in the second decade of the century. Comic opera began in 1728 with John Gay's *Beggars' Opera*, which never exhausted its popularity throughout the century. The puppet theatre, elaborate and simple, drew crowds of adults as well as children. The theatre of varieties, the ancestor of the nineteenth-century music hall, proved a broader, grosser source of enjoyment than the genteel plays the straight theatre offered. Nor were the working classes deprived of theatrical entertainment; crude melodramas drew them in hundreds to the village barns, though the consequences could occasionally be fatal: nearly two hundred were incinerated at a performance at Burwell in Cambridgeshire.

The popularity of the theatre and of its leading actors was immense, and naturally enough print sellers and artists exploited their opportunity. The Prince Regent, afterwards George IV, collected, as a young man, every print of David Garrick he could lay his hands on – he bought one hundred and fifty. Similarly theatre scenes made popular pictures and were quickly engraved. Excellent artists throughout the century painted the landscapes and scenes from urban life for the floats in which the audiences took so much delight. Indeed, the theatre, now neatly framed by the proscenium arch, became a living picture, and a permanent part of social life. It was commercially important too, for it projected what was chic in dress and manners and style of living.

Thomas Rowlandson *Punch and Judy Show*, c. 1800–20.

William Hogarth *Children Playing 'The Indian Emperor'*, 1731–32.

William Hogarth *The Beggar's Opera.*

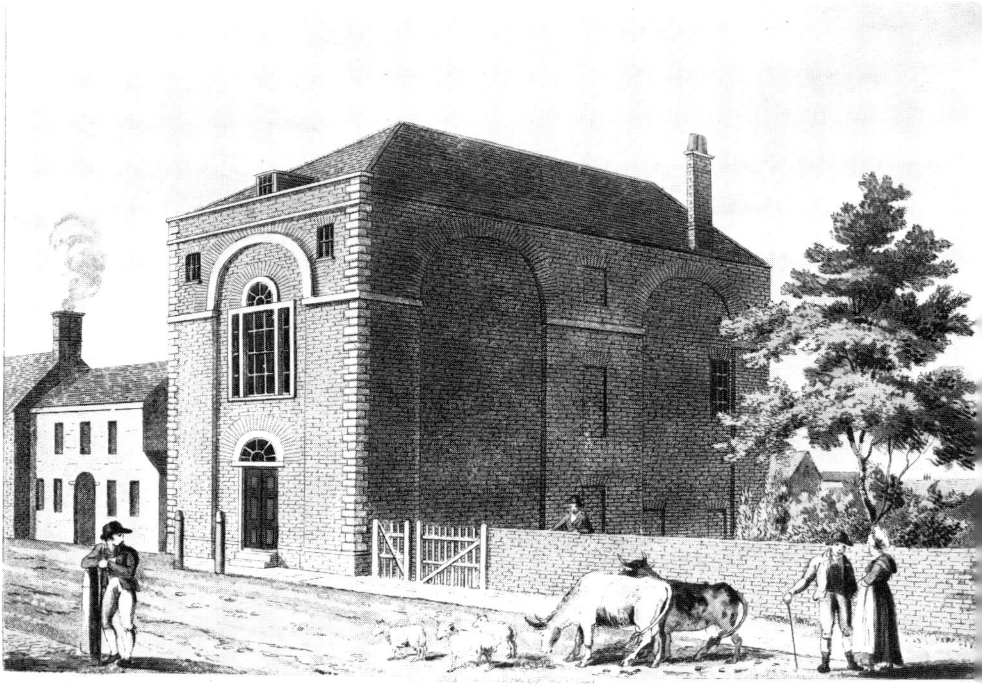

GRANTHAM.

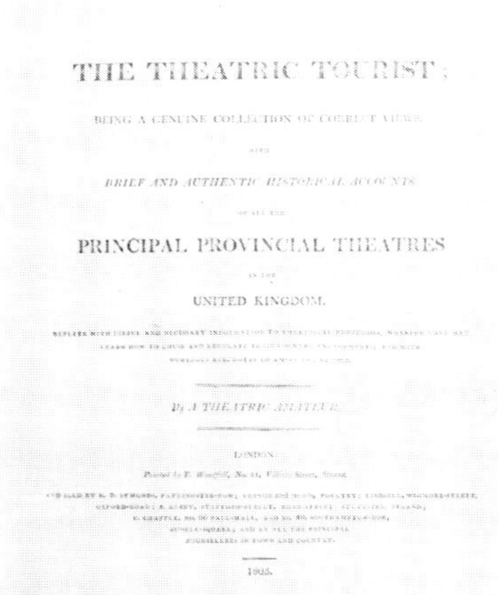

THE THEATRIC TOURIST;

BEING A GENUINE COLLECTION OF CORRECT VIEWS,

WITH

BRIEF AND AUTHENTIC HISTORICAL ACCOUNTS

OF ALL THE

PRINCIPAL PROVINCIAL THEATRES

IN THE

UNITED KINGDOM.

By A THEATRIC AMATEUR.

LONDON:

1805.

TOP *Grantham Theatre* from James Winston's *The Theatric Tourist*, 1805.

ABOVE LEFT Title page from *The Theatric Tourist*.

ABOVE RIGHT George Dance *A Man Doing Splits*, 1760–90.

TOP A. Van Assen *The Italian Theatre, Haymarket.*

ABOVE Engraving of the interior of the first Theatre Royal, Drury Lane; built by Henry Holland, it was destroyed by fire in 1809.

# *Music*

There is considerable irony about the development of music in eighteenth-century England. Although its audience was large, indeed larger than in any other country in Europe, the eighteenth century produced fewer composers of genius than either the sixteenth or the seventeenth centuries had done. Thomas Arne and William Boyce were, it is true, very good musicians, but not of compelling genius. English music was dominated by Handel, who settled in England in Queen Anne's reign. His oratorios, particularly *The Messiah*, achieved a national popularity that has rarely, if ever, been equalled by a composer of serious music in Britain. He was the favourite of the amateur choir, which sprang up in many provincial towns in Britain, and when two great commemorative celebrations of Handel were arranged in Westminster Abbey (1784) and York Minster (1823), they drew thousands of spectators.

London was without a regular concert hall in the seventeenth century, but by 1750 a number of large halls, where Londoners first heard the music of Bach, Mozart and Haydn, had been built. Foreign composers and performers were in great demand. Italy provided almost a regiment of singers, whose popularity never diminished. So large was the demand to hear Signor Noferi sing at a concert in Cambridge that the innkeepers were forced to ration beds.

The stimulus of so many brilliant public concerts encouraged amateur performers, and so created a demand for printed music and for instruments upon which to play it. Scores were very cheap, so were many instruments, which could be hired for a small weekly sum. Music masters – rare in seventeenth-century England – everywhere abounded, making a handsome living from the aspirations of the middle classes, for musical accomplishment was regarded as particularly genteel, especially for girls. So was dancing – not only refined forms of country dancing, but also the new styles from Europe. It trained both boys and girls in deportment, and the way one moved in the eighteenth century was a badge of one's social class: to walk clumsily, to make an awkward bow could be highly embarrassing. On nights of the full moon coaches and horses clattered towards the inns and assembly rooms of towns great and small, where attorneys, prosperous farmers and shopkeepers who had subscribed for the balls danced the night away. A new world of sound and song and dancing had come into being.

Marcellus Laroon *A Concert at Montague House.*

By Music minds an equal temper know;
Nor swell too high nor sink too low;
HARMONY and SENTIMENT.
" Warriors she fires with animated
" Pours balm into the bleeding lovers

LEFT, ABOVE Philippe Mercier *Frederick, Prince of Wales and his Sisters: A Music Party*, 1733.

FAR LEFT Thomas Hudson *George Frederick Handel*, 1756.

LEFT Etching after Bartolozzi of Thomas Arne.

ABOVE Johann Zoffany *The Sharp Family*, 1779–80.

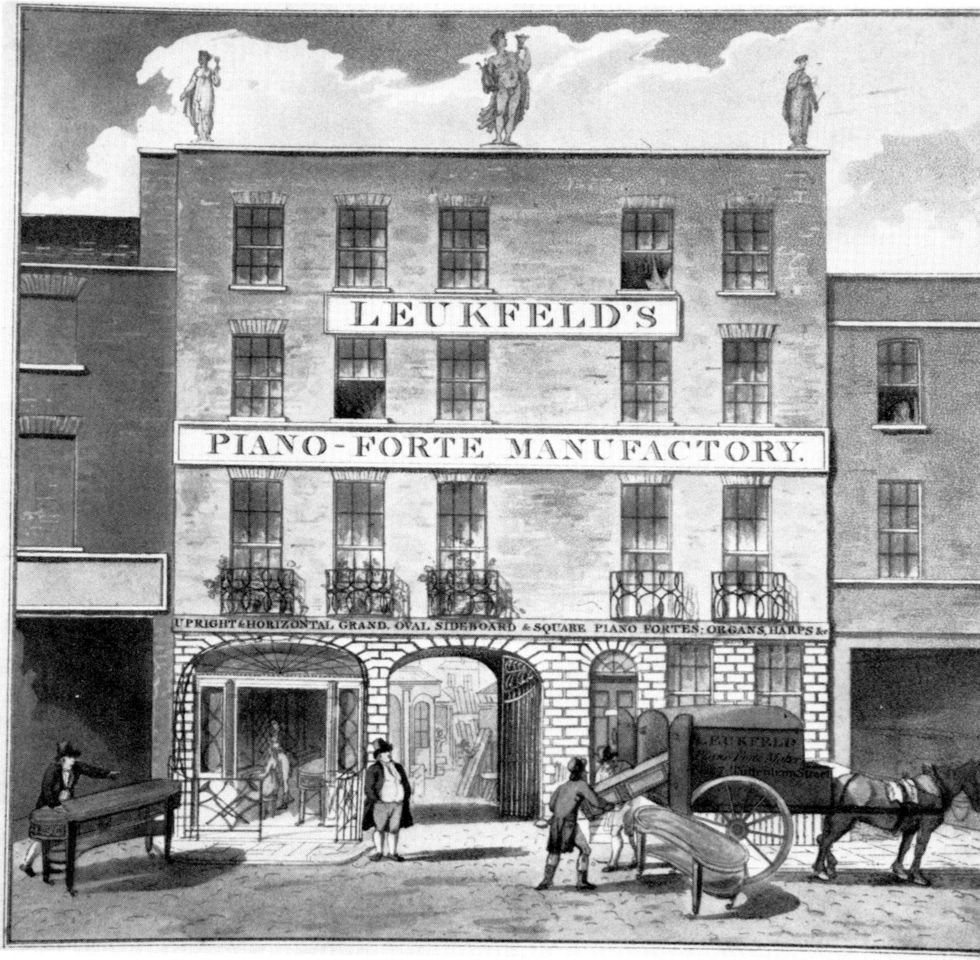


ABOVE Trade card of Ludwig Leukfeld, piano maker, c. 1798.

RIGHT Trade card of Miss Dietrichsen, harp, piano and singing teacher, c. 1798.

On moderate Terms,

THE HARP,

PIANO FORTE & SINGING,

*Taught by*

*Miss Dietrichsen,*

*12, Rathbone Place,*

*Oxford Street.*

White, Engraver, 14, Brownlow Street, Holborn.

Hen: Morland pinx! Published as the Act directs. A.D. 1769. Phil: Dawe fec.

The pretty Ballad Singer.

7

Printed for CARINGTON BOWLES, Map & Printseller, No. 69 in St. Pauls Church Yard, LONDON.

LEFT Mezzotint after Henry Morland *The pretty Ballad Singer*, 1769.

ABOVE Thomas Rowlandson *The Concert Singers*, c. 1785–1800.

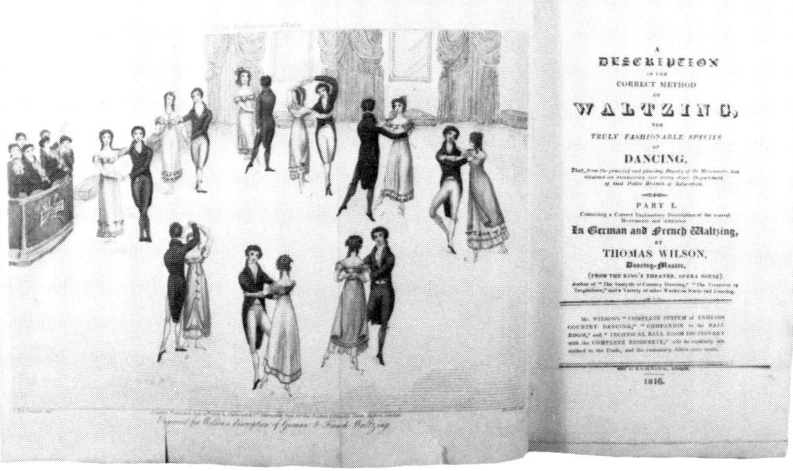

TOP Frontispiece and title page from *A Description of the Correct Method of Waltzing* by Thomas Wilson, 1816.

ABOVE Anon *Home-made Entertainment in the Drawing-Room*, c. 1810.

TOP David Allan *The Halkett Family Group*, 1781.

ABOVE Sir David Wilkie *The Penny Wedding*, 1818.

# *Art*

English painting in the seventeenth century had been far less remarkable than music or literature. Apart from Dobson and the miniaturists, there were few English artists of great distinction. Hilliard, the Olivers and Cooper had created a magnificent tradition of jewel-like painting, perceptive of mood and alert to character, that is the most original feature of British seventeenth-century art. The Court had been dominated by a succession of Netherlandish or German painters from Holbein to Kneller, and the great connoisseurs had not paid much regard to British artists. Architecture was a different matter: Jones, Webb, Wren, Hawksmoor and finally Vanburgh had created a magnificent native tradition, firmly based on the great classical heritage but capable of originality and in a style that was entirely English. In the eighteenth century architecture moved closer to the classical European manner, based on Rome and Greece, whereas painting in England developed its own distinctive school, aware surely of the great achievements of Italy, France and the Netherlands, but master of its own idiom.

The market for paintings in the seventeenth century had been small; it was strongest in portraiture, for the country gentry as well as the more sophisticated members of the Court and aristocracy wished to be recorded for posterity, but the provincial painters whom most of them employed were inept – often self-taught and of little experience. In the eighteenth century this market grew rapidly and the response was far more professional; in Hogarth Britain produced its first painter of outstanding genius, an artist of exceptional range and power, but he was quickly matched, if not surpassed, by Reynolds and Gainsborough. Not far behind came a stream of portrait painters of the highest distinction, from Arthur Devis to Sir Thomas Lawrence.

Equally impressive was the diversity of English painting. Hogarth himself painted theatre scenes, historical pictures and what proved to be of quite exceptional popularity – his contemporary history pictures such as *The Rake's Progress*. Landscape and animal painting were combined in the huge, bold and superbly decorative canvases of John Wootton. Indeed, animal painting flourished in England as nowhere else, culminating in the superb pictures of horses and foals of George Stubbs. Richard Wilson and Samuel Scott revealed their exceptional talent in landscapes and scenes or urban life.

The Hanoverian dynasty, contrary to common belief, exercised a wise and discerning patronage. George I patronised William Kent. His grandson Frederick, Prince of Wales, was a very great collector as well as patron. George III never missed an exhibition at the Royal Academy, which he founded, and he was also an accomplished watercolourist. His son George IV was the greatest connoisseur – after Charles I – to sit on the English throne.

Plentiful as paintings were, they were too costly for the masses. Their needs were met by the development of the engraving. Hogarth, as great an entrepreneur as Josiah Wedgwood, secured a copyright act which made prints very valuable to the artist himself. Prints of contemporary events, of modern and old masters, satires of social life and politics, filled shops which often sold nothing else, so great was the demand. Some families, like Mrs Thrale's, actually papered their walls with them.

As with music, so with painting, particularly watercolours; it became a genteel art, thought to be particularly appropriate for young gentlewomen, and drawing masters were to be found throughout the provinces. Teaching aids, some very beautiful books in their own right, were produced for the same purpose – to teach people to paint flowers or landscapes. And this widespread emphasis on the teaching of art had two other social purposes. One was to encourage young men to draw with exactitude, a very desirable skill in many new professions, particularly surveying and engineering. As the industrial revolution developed, the demand for artistic competence grew, not only for young men but also for young women, in the manufacture of porcelain, textiles, wallpapers and the like. Design was of prime importance. The other purpose was moral: a careful portrayal of nature – of flowers, of insects, of animals, of skies and winds and clouds – gave a deeper insight into the beauty of God's creation. As so often in the eighteenth century, the delight of the eye was linked with the improvement of the mind and the heart.

ABOVE Plate 3 from William Hogarth's *The Rake's Progress*, 1735.

RIGHT George Shepherd *York House with Richardson's Ancient and Modern Print Warehouse*, c. 1809.

YORKHOUSE
Richardson ancient & modern Print WAREHOUS

ABOVE Engraving after H. Ramberg *The Exhibition of the Royal Academy, 1787.*

RIGHT Thomas Gainsborough *The Hon. Mrs Graham, 1775.*

LEFT Francis Cotes *Paul Sandby*, 1761.

BELOW, LEFT Title page from *Introduction to The Art of Drawi*
by G. Bickham, 1735.

BELOW, RIGHT Plate 2 from *A*
*Introduction to The Art of Drawing*.

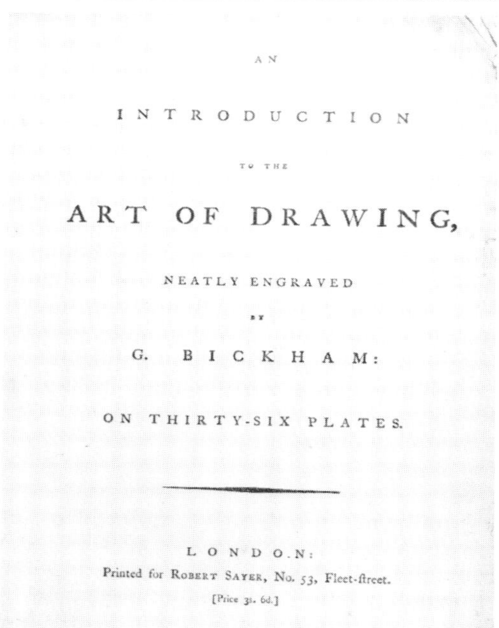

AN

INTRODUCTION

TO THE

ART OF DRAWING,

NEATLY ENGRAVED

BY

G. BICKHAM:

ON THIRTY-SIX PLATES.

LONDON:
Printed for ROBERT SAYER, No. 53, Fleet-ſtreet.
[Price 3s. 6d.]

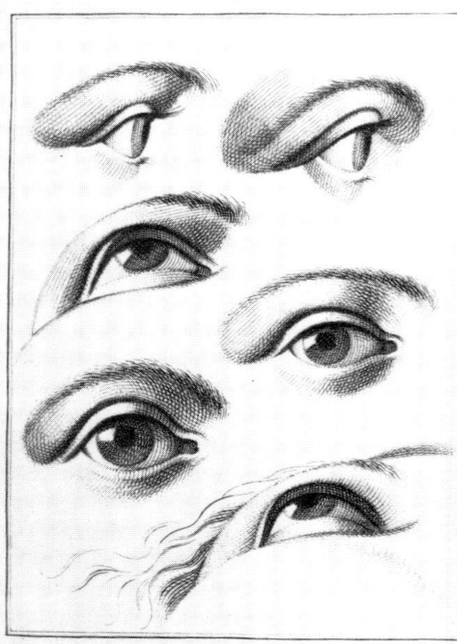

TOP Trade card advertising sketches by George Morland, 1801.

ABOVE Trade card of S. and I. Fuller used as an advertisement in *The Ladies Magazine*, August 1823.

# *The Beauty of Creation*

The theology of the eighteenth century stressed the rationality of the universe, that although God's ways might be mysterious, there was, behind all experience, a grand design. 'Whatever is, is right.' Also many believed that the closer one observed nature, the more one became aware of the beauties of God's creation. There were two instruments that were at the same time scientific, moral, and, in a sense, theological: the orrery, which displayed the great macrocosm – the universe with its ordered stars and planets moving on their destined and regular courses – and the microscope, which revealed the delicate mechanism, the surprising beauty and vivid colours of the microcosm, invisible to the human eye.

More men, and not merely scholars, began to observe nature closely; birds, animals, flowers, the formation of rocks, the passage of clouds, the effects of light and wind entranced them and stimulated their desire for accuracy and understanding. Those skilled in words, like Gilbert White of Selbourne, described with perception the living world about them. Mark Catesby spent years in Virginia and the Carolinas painting with exquisite accuracy their flora and fauna. Rarely before had flowers been painted with such beautiful precision; neither had the strange exotic animals which were, at this time, brought to England – all a part of the great unfolding drama of creation.

Strange animals, rare plants, exotic birds excited great curiosity. The botanical gardens at Kew were created to bring together the new vast world of rare trees, shrubs and flowers. Somewhat later the royal collection of animals – many, like the llama, the kangaroo and the giraffe, novel to England – became the foundation of the London Zoo.

Naturally it was not only the sight of animals that aroused curiosity, but also the way they were made, the way they worked as living mechanisms – hence the anatomy of animals became a subject of intense interest.

Men of more analytic cast of mind wished to probe into the secrets of the universe. George III was very interested in the stars. As a young man he built his own observatory and later patronized the astronomer Herschel, and built larger and larger telescopes for him. And Herschel repaid him by discovering more distant planets and remoter stars. Others, using their technical ingenuity, investigated the mysterious properties of electricity, and lectured about them to large and curious audiences.

Experiment led to invention, which was also stimulated by the growing market for goods of all kinds. There was little direct connection between scientific revolution and the industrial inventions which did so much to stimulate production, but both were a part of the same intellectual climate. At all levels of society men were fascinated by nature and experiment, whether it was Joseph Priestley in his laboratory, or a humble shopkeeper trying to breed a more exotic carnation, a faster pigeon or a tougher bulldog. The more that was discovered, the deeper men penetrated into the material world, the more beautiful did God's creation seem to the seeker. At this time even geology fortified religion rather than undermined it for what could be clearer evidence of the Flood than sea shells on a mountain top?

Lithograph by James Hakewill *Monkey House in the Zoological Gardens*, 1831.

LEFT Engraving showing th forty-foot telescope designe by William Hershel and dedicated to George III, 1775.

BELOW Julius Caesar Ibbetson *The Ascent of Lunardi's Balloon from St George's Fields*, c. 1788–90.

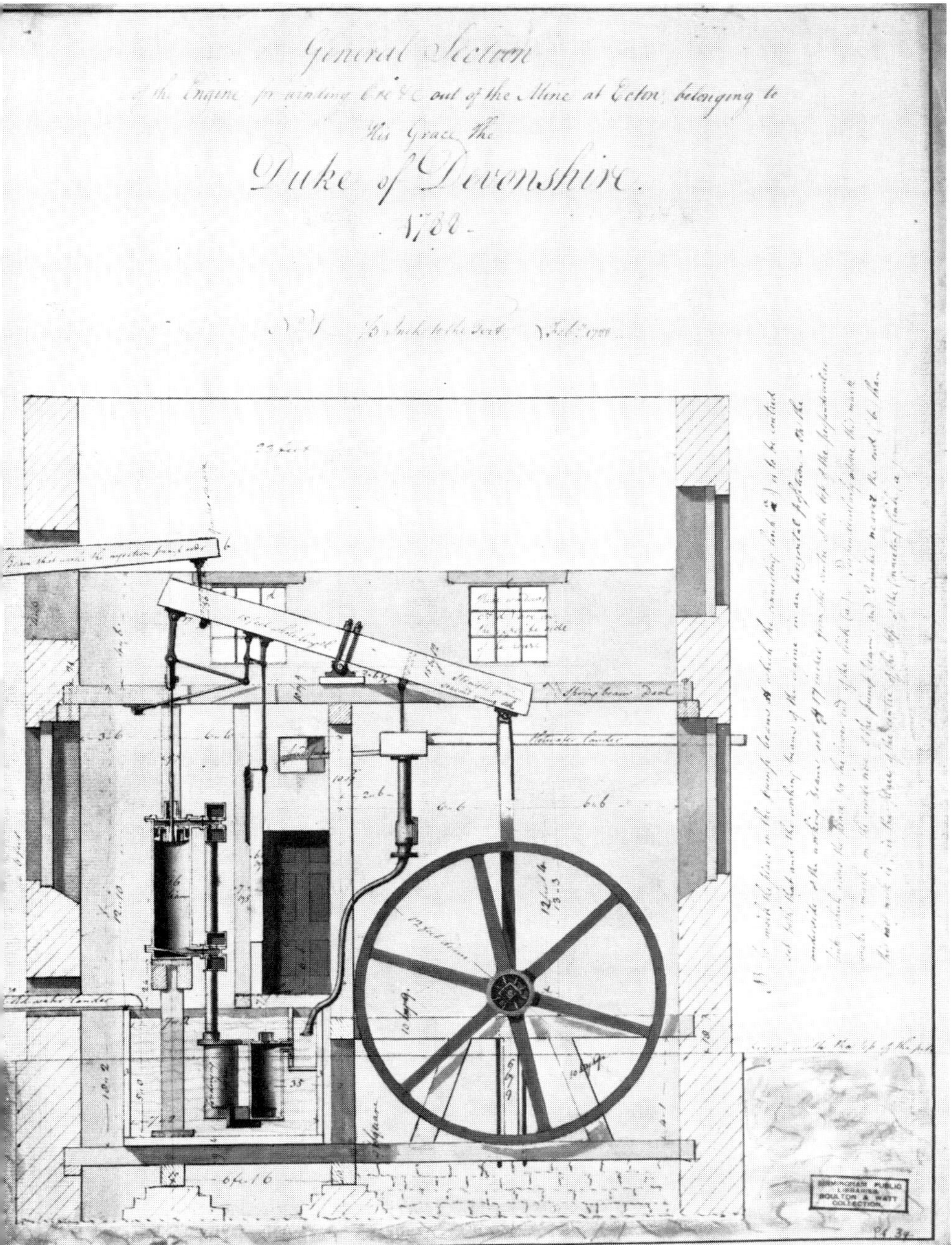


Section drawing of the Watt Engine, 1788.

ABOVE Trade card of Thomas Wright, mathematical instrument-maker to George III, advertising the Great Orrery.

RIGHT Trade card of R. Rust, inventor and retailer of scientific instruments.

INVENTED & MADE by R, RUST,
Removed from ye MINORIES to the Corner of
St. CATHERINES STAIRS. Near
the TOWER of LONDON
AN ARTIFICIAL HORRIZON
To be Used When the Real Horrizon
Is Thick & Obscure Or Instead of
The Back Observation

Painted by JOSEPH WRIGHT, R.A. 1790. Engraved by I.R.SMITH, Mezzotinto Engraver to H.R.H. the Prince of Wales, May 5, 1

Sr. Richard Arkwright

LEFT Engraving after Joseph Wright of Derby *Sir Richard Arkwright*, inventor of the Spinning Jenny, 1801.

ABOVE S. Slaughter *Sir Hans Sloane*, physician and collector, 1736.

ABOVE Ramsay Richard Reinagle *John Latham (?) Examining a Bird of Paradise*, c. 1800–10.

RIGHT Drawing by George Stubbs *The Anatomy of the Horse*, 1766.

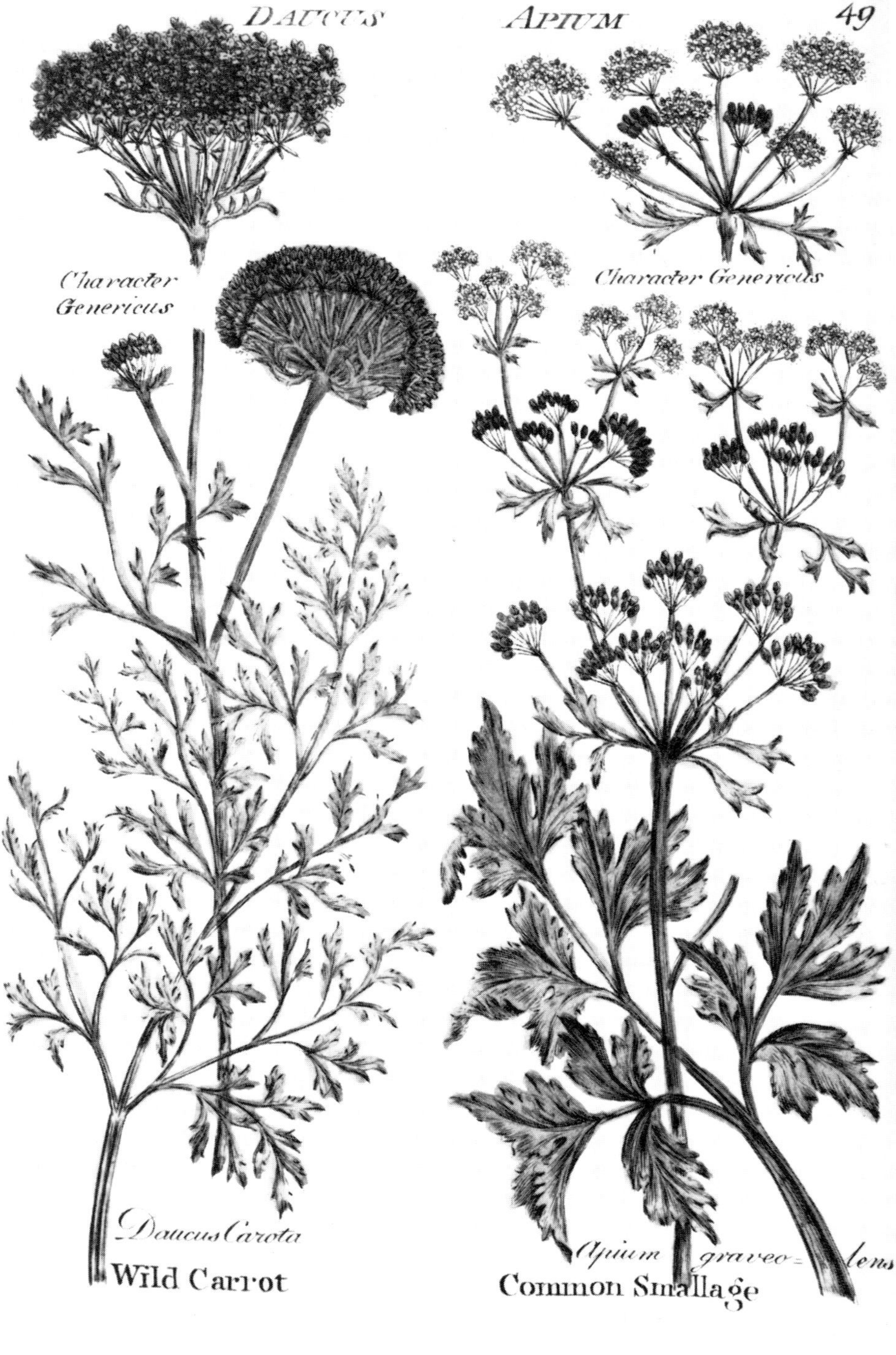
DAUCUS
APIUM
Character Genericus
Character Genericus
Daucus Carota
Wild Carrot
Apium graveolens
Common Smallage

LEFT Page from *Culpeper's Works*, Volume III, 1802.

ABOVE Frontispiece to the catalogue of the Portland Museum, 1786.

# *Racing*

The eighteenth century witnessed the development of horse-racing as we know it today; it was the first great commercialized sport that England gave to the world. The Stuart kings had patronized the turf; Queen Anne, another great supporter of racing, initiated Royal Ascot. Even so, racing was something of a haphazard affair, even in 1715; frequently it was a matter of wagers between gentlemen, their horses often ridden by themselves, occasionally with a royal or a gold cup to race for, but there was little organization of the racing calendar or of the rules of racing.

By 1800 all had changed. The breeding of horses had developed almost beyond recognition. The great racing stallions and mares were public figures as well known as David Garrick or Handel.

Races as well as horses improved. The calendar was systematized so that there was less conflict between important meetings. Information about the going and the winners of important races was widely disseminated. One of the reasons for the success of the provincial newspaper was the fact that it carried news not only of local races but of distant ones, often as far as one hundred and fifty miles away. Professional trainers became widespread and the use of professional jockeys almost universal; the rules of racing were closely defined and more strictly enforced by the Jockey Club of Newmarket, which became recognized in Ireland as well as Britain as the final authority on all disputes. Even so, it remained a corrupt sport. Chicanery of all kinds was difficult to suppress when so much money was at stake. Even George IV's jockey was discovered to have fixed a race.

Chicanery or not, the public interest in racing grew with the passing years and crowds increased. Early in the century grand-stands had been built to accommodate the richer clients who wished to get away from the mob, drunks, gambling, even whoring. Heavy capital was invested in racecourses, as well as in stud farms and the horses themselves.

The success of British racing was universally acknowledged; well known winners were exported in the first instance to Virginia, and afterwards to the rest of the American colonies. Races in America were conducted on British lines. France, too, adopted British methods and imported most of its bloodstock from Britain. So popular a sport provided an active field of interest for artists and engravers. Pictures of popular horses and popular jockeys were to be found in every print shop. Naturally owners wanted their great winners immortalized, and Wootton, Herring and George Stubbs painted the outstanding racehorses of Georgian England. There were also plenty of provincial painters willing to do a quick likeness of a gentleman's winner for a four or five guinea fee, and one artist in York advertised his skill at providing portraits in stained glass. Certainly racing was the first sport to be fully professionalized, to become what was, in effect, an industry and to draw a mass audience.

English School *The Godolphin Arabian.*

BETTING ROOM
GODOLPHIN.
THE JOCKEY CLUB OR NEWMARKET MEETING.

LEFT, ABOVE English School *Epsom stand at Newmarket*, early nineteenth century.

LEFT Thomas Rowlandson *The Jockey Club or Newmarket Meeting*, 1824.

TOP Thomas Rowlandson *The Road to Epsom*, 1812.

ABOVE Thomas Rowlandson *Racing at Newmarket*.

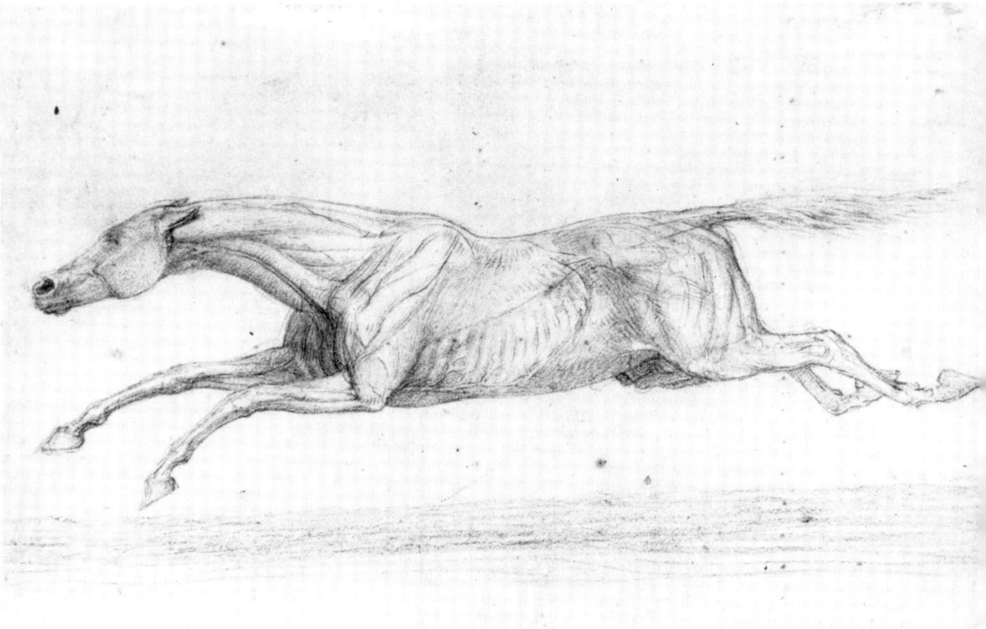

LEFT, ABOVE Drawing by George Stubbs *A Racehorse in Action.*

LEFT George Stubbs *Gimcrack on Newmarket Heath,* 1765.

ABOVE Engraving by John Sartorius *The Derby Sweepstake,* 1791–92.

# *Sports*

Although horse-racing dominated the sporting scene, the eighteenth-century gentleman possessed the choice of a large variety of sports and games. If he was of a sedentary nature, there were chess and billiards, both quite ancient games, but both developed considerably in the eighteenth century; more and more people played both games, new techniques were invented and produced players of quite exceptional skill and public notoriety. For aggressive men, who preferred to watch rather than participate, boxing provided a tough, bloody, highly professional sport. During the century it developed from the art of self-defence into a spectacle, promoted by sharp-eyed entrepreneurs who made fortunes for themselves and for their leading boxers. Boxing, like racing, was big business. Although opposed by many earnest evangelists, the populace adored the sport for it matched the mood of an aggressive society.

Equally popular with those who played as well as watched was cricket, a complex game, ideal for betting, that drew noblemen and yeomen together in a common pursuit. Cricket, too, became steadily professionalized and organized into a spectator-orientated sport – with catering franchises being sold at big matches by the middle of the century.

Many men, however, preferred to pursue their sporting activities alone or with a few friends. Sailing for pleasure, or, at times, racing in competitions, was widespread, naturally enough in a seafaring nation; the inland waters as well as the sea coasts were alive with the sails of pleasure craft. The third Earl of Orford, wildly eccentric, built a splendid yacht and dubbed himself Admiral of the Fens. He and the Earl of Sandwich ran regattas on Whittlesea Mere. And it was a sport that many ladies as well as gentlemen enjoyed. Orford's mistress, Patty Turk, was always on board his yacht.

Great improvements in sporting guns made it possible to shoot birds on the wing with more than a fair chance of success if the eye was keen and the arm steady. As well as providing excellent sport, the birds also stocked the larder with delectable game. In consequence, shooting rights were carefully protected, the game laws savage and poaching universal.

And so it was with the hunting of deer. The royal foresters and the gentry who possessed large deer parks did their utmost to protect their venison. The laws against poaching deer – or rabbits for that matter – were exceptionally savage, but rarely deterred the organized bands of poachers who resented the forest laws, and were willing to risk their necks for the profits they made. Such considerations did not enter the sport that became the most popular of all in the eighteenth century – fox-hunting. In the previous century it had been largely a sport for farmers and the occasional large landowner with his own pack of hounds, but now it developed into a highly organized, expensive sport to which many fox-hunting men became addicts for life. They were exhilarated by fast, dangerous runs in the open country of the English Midlands, with its rolling hills, quick-set hedges and deep ditches – death traps to the unwary. Breeding produced the key to success with hounds as with horses. Not surprisingly Robert Bakewell, who produced the best cattle, was a close friend of Francis Meynell who produced the best hounds, both Leicestershire men.

Old sports were transmogrified, new ones developed; some ancient pastimes – especially of the more sadistic kind – were suppressed, but some, too, were revived. In the seventeenth century archery was almost moribund, but the eighteenth century witnessed its revival; indeed it was a unique sport in that ladies and gentleman could compete against each other, and it became very popular in the great country houses. It possessed the further charm of reminding participants and viewers of the victories of England, particularly Agincourt, in the centuries long past.

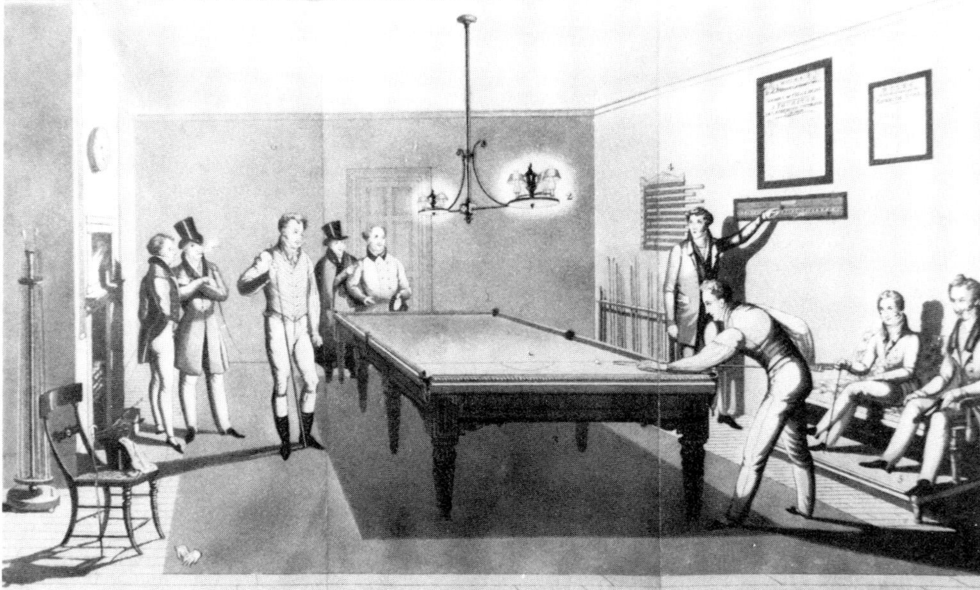

1. A Circular Cue Rack. 2. A Newly invented revolving Lamp. 3. A Billiard Table. 4. A Pool Marking board. 5. A high Seat.

J. THURSTON, MANUFACTURER, 14, CATHERINE STREET, STRAND, LONDON.

FAR LEFT Thomas Rowlandson *Checkmate*, c. 1785–95.

FAR LEFT, BELOW Frontispiece from *The Noble Game of Billiards* by Mingaud, 1830.

LEFT Anon *Gentleman John Jackson*, pugilist.

BELOW Thomas Rowlandson *The Prize Fight*, 1787.

TOP Anon *A Game of Cricket*, 1790.

ABOVE English School *Yachts of the Cumberland Fleet starting at Blackfriars*, late eighteenth century.

TOP Thomas Rowlandson *Fishing*.

ABOVE Julius Caesar Ibbetson *Skating in Hyde Park*, c. 1785.

Engraving after Adam Buck *Archers*, 1799.

TOP George Smith *Winter Landscape with Hunter.*
ABOVE Francis Hayman *Thomas Nuthall and his friend Hambleton Custance,* 1748.

TOP James Seymour *A Kill at Ashdown Park*, 1743.

ABOVE Charles Loraine Smith *Dick Knight of the Pytchley*, 1790.

TOP Etching by Thomas Rowlandson *The Return*, 1788.

ABOVE George Stubbs *The Grosvenor Hunt*, 1762.

# *The Discovery of Britain*

Large scale travel for the pleasure of travelling or in order to broaden the mind was a development of the eighteenth century. The shipping lanes along the coasts were full of small vessels, often carrying passengers (if the winds were favourable this was much the quickest route between Edinburgh and London). The new canals which began to criss-cross the land after 1760 carried people as well as goods in specially designed barges. But most who could afford it went by coach, either public or private, a method which improved immeasurably during the century. Others rode their own horses or hired one. Some hardy spirits, like the young writer William Hazlitt, walked for fun or, like David Garrick seeking fame in London, from necessity.

The flow of travellers, naturally led to a greater concern with the mechanics of travel, to developments which would increase speed and secure greater comfort. In consequence, there was a great deal of experimentation in the design of carriages: a lower centre of gravity was required to prevent overturning; leaf springs, first of leather and then of steel, made the jolting less intolerable, as did improvements in the engineering, draining and surfacing of roads. Speed was greatly helped by the breeding of a strong but fast horse, the Cleveland Bay, which was very suitable for coach work. The boom in canal building removed a great deal of heavy traffic from the roads, which helped to preserve their surfaces from the very deep rutting which had been the bane of early decades. The skilful engineering techniques of Macadam and Telford improved gradients and drainage. By 1820 movement about England was fast and cheap, faster and cheaper, in fact, than ever before in history but, even so, it was too expensive for the poorer classes. They walked. Their day came with the railway and the cheap excursion fare, invented by Thomas Cook in the 1850s. By then the great stage-coach era had come to an end. The passing of the stage-coach had a crippling effect on the country inn, which had blossomed in response to the increased travelling in the eighteenth century. Many coaching inns were vast and splendid. They competed vigorously with each other, offering enticing bargains – newly wainscotted rooms, exhibitions, lectures, subscription concerts, and, of course, superior stabling. Many of these inns clung to a precarious life until they were revived once more with the coming of the automobile. Many of the great inns, such as the Bear at Woodstock or the Lygon Arms at Broadway, remain as gracious now as they were two hundred years ago.

Increasingly people travelled to see sights, to satisfy their curiosity about their country and its past. Those who could afford it went in their own coaches, others by the rapidly improving stage-coach. Travel began to intensify after 1760 when visits to the mountainous parts of Britain – Wales, the Lake District and Scotland – became very popular. The mountains deeply stirred the emotions; special vantage points were built so that travellers could – for a small fee – sit and contemplate a particularly sublime view of mountain, lake and cascade. Pleasure boats cruised the lakes and anchored under the more awesome cliffs; landscape and the emotions it aroused were carefully orchestrated, and the sublime became an almost banal cliché. Underneath it all was a strong moral theme that reached back to classical Roman antiquity: the contrast between the corrupt city and the virtuous countryside.

Ruins possessed a similar virtue. They spoke not only of England's glorious past – of Romans, Druids, medieval kings, and of the old Catholic faith – but also, like the landscapes, they spoke a metaphysical language which the travellers were trained to listen to. They spoke of the transience of all things; they taught that nothing can withstand the hand of Time; that even the proudest works of men are humbled. Above all they underlined the smallness of man, the fragility of his hopes and ambitions when set in the framework of eternity. Ruins were endowed with moral virtue.

Certainly people travelled to be morally uplifted, but they also travelled to satisfy their curiosity and to see how other people lived, especially those richer than themselves. Like English people today, eighteenth-century men and women were passionate country house visitors, willingly paying their five shillings to the housekeeper of Chatsworth, which has always been open to the public, to see the wonders of the Duke of Devonshire's art collection or to be allowed to wander in the beauty of his new garden. They would just as willingly make a detour to view the new industrial wonders of their age. As exciting as climbing a mountain was the descent in an iron cage into the depths of a coal mine. Never before had so many people seen so much of Britain and its wonders, ancient and modern.

ABOVE Thomas Rowlandson *Old Elephant and Castle Inn, Newington.*

RIGHT, ABOVE J. Cordrey *The London to Dartford Stage Coach*, 1813.

RIGHT Trade card advertising the Ram Inn at Cirencester, designed by William Hogarth, 1719.

JOHN & RICHARD WEAVER.
NEAT
Post-Chaises,
LANDAU
& Landaulet,
WITH
CAREFUL
DRIVERS.
JOHN SHAW RAM INN CIRENCESTER
CHOICE
Old Wines,
GOOD
Stabling &
LOCK UP
COACH
HOUSES.
Copied from the Original (now in possession of Mr. Philip Watkins, Cirencester)
and Engraved by Edw. Power, Gloucester.

ABOVE Antonio Canaletto *Interior of Henry* VII*'s Chapel, Westminster Abbey,* c. 1750.

RIGHT The main staircase at Montague House, then the British Museum, early nineteenth century.

FAR LEFT, ABOVE George Garrard *The Eighth Duke of Hamilton Riding Along the Shore.*

FAR LEFT George Barret *A View of Powerscourt*, c. 1755–60.

ABOVE Engraving after C. Catton *A View of Jedburgh Abbey*, 1793.

LEFT Bill from the Tontine Inn showing the Iron Bridge, 1797.

*The Most Noble Francis Egerton,* Duke of Bridgewater;
*and* Marquis *of* Brackley.
*Seu Navis Brittannæ Magister.*
*Magnificum pretiosus emptor.*

LEFT Engraving of the Duke of Bridgewater, canal builder.

ABOVE Ackermann print of the Liverpool–Manchester Railway excavation works, 1831.

# The World Beyond

Travel has liberated human beings for time out of mind. Even in the fifth century AD rich Roman ladies were visiting Mount Sinai and its hermits; and throughout the Middle Ages men and women combined a pilgrimage with the delight of seeing foreign lands. The discovery of America had stimulated greater excitement and confirmed the belief that there were new worlds to discover. By the eighteenth century, the Englishman's knowledge of the globe was almost complete; some geographical details, especially of the Pacific, were still lacking, but by 1800 the outlines of the continents and the oceans were known. Englishmen were everywhere – for the purpose of trade, for missionary enterprise, for sheer curiosity. Also, more young Britons had begun to travel, particularly in Europe, and to travel with a definitive purpose – cultural education.

The rich, mainly the elder sons of the aristocracy and gentry, were sent to make the Grand Tour – mainly to France, Italy and the Netherlands – to acquire a knowledge of languages, to learn the usages of sophisticated European society and develop a taste for architecture and the arts, which, since the Renaissance, had been thought to be the proper attribute of a gentleman. Young aristocrats bent on a career in diplomacy or war had travelled to Europe to learn languages or the latest developments in fortifications or tactics during the sixteenth and seventeenth centuries, but the bold spirits had been few in number. Most gentlemen were educated in England. But from 1690 the mood of the aristocracy began to change: three or four years spent in Europe came to be regarded as essential for the truly polished young man. Indeed the Society of Dilettanti was formed so that young men who had been to Italy could meet and maintain their mutual interests. One of the major purposes of the Grand Tour was to acquire an understanding of the arts – painting, sculpture, architecture and music – which their parents believed was best acquired in Italy.

As well as artistic culture the aristocrat on the Grand Tour was expected to learn languages, especially French, the lingua franca of polite society throughout Europe. So popular had the Grand Tour become that all the paraphernalia of modern travel had been brought into being by the 1760s including guides to historical monuments and art galleries. In Rome there were permanent resident Britons who would act as guides or as advisers on artistic purchases. Some were not above swindling their clients, selling them dubious antiquities and getting a cut from seller as well as buyer. Few young aristocrats returned without crates of art and antiques with which to adorn their country homes, sometimes of the highest quality, sometimes fake. There is not a region of England that could not mount a fascinating exhibition from its country houses of paintings and objects acquired on the Grand Tour. This singular and expensive education bred, nevertheless, a respect for artistic life. Like so many other pursuits of the eighteenth century, these pleasures of foreign travel began to be enjoyed by more than the aristocracy. By 1800 young middle-class Englishmen, like Wordsworth, were beginning to tramp the roads of France and Italy with packs strapped to their backs. Their parents, too, often took short holidays in France. Spinsters of delicate health and modest incomes, retired army and naval officers, were beginning to form small English colonies in Florence, in Venice, in Nice and on the Riviera. They were the vanguard of the mass travel of the nineteenth and twentieth centuries.

A few adventurous spirits, even amongst the young aristocrats on the Grand Tour, had ventured further than France, Italy and the Netherlands. The young Lord Herbert, with his excellent tutor William Coxe, had explored Poland and Russia before returning to England. The young Byron and his friend Cam Hobhouse visited Greece, Turkey and the Middle East, much to the enrichment of his poetry, if not of his morals. The world beyond the immediate confines of Europe, however, was rarely visited except by traders, soldiers, sailors and missionaries. Yet by 1820 there were quite large pockets of English society in India, Canton, South Africa and Australia. Young and not so young artists – like George Chinery and Tilly Kettle – followed, painting portraits, the strange landscapes and the exotic animals. India naturally attracted more artists than anywhere else because of the large British communities in Calcutta and Madras.

And the extension of the new and growing British empire excited the imagination of those at home, who bought eagerly the beautifully illustrated travel books that were so marked a feature of British publishing between 1800 and 1830, works of art, indeed, in themselves. They looked magnificent on library tables specially designed for them. The coffee-table book fulfils the same function for a mass society but with less elegance, less beauty.

The IMPORTS of GREAT BRITAIN from FRANCE.

*Humbly Addrefs'd to the laudable Afsociations of Anti-Gallicans, and the generous promoters of the British Arts & Manufactories by their sincere Well-wisher, and truly devoted humble Servant, L.P. Boitard*

*Invented & Engraved by L.P. Boitard.* **EXPLANATION.** *Four Tackle Porters staggering under a weighty Chest of* **Birth Night Cloaths.** *Behind, several emaciated high liv'd Epicures, familiarly receiving a* **French Cook**, *acquainting him that without his Afsistance they must have Perish'd with Hunger. — A Lady of Distinction, offering the tuition of her Son & Daughter to a cringing* **French Abbe**, *disregarding the Corruption of their Religion, so they do but obtain the true French Accent, her Frenchified well-bred Spouse readily complying. — The English Chaplain regretting his lost Labours. Another Woman of Quality in Raptures, carefsing a* **French Female Dancer**, *afsuring her that her Arrival is to the* **Honour & Delight of England.** *On the front ground a Cask overset; the Contents,* **French Cheeses**, *from Normandy bein[illegible] Raffraicts, a Black Guard Boy stopping his Nostrils greatly offended at the Haut Gout. A Chest well cramm'd with Toppets, Mafks, Ribands, Flowers for the Hair, & other such* **Material Bagatelles**, *underneath, conceal'd* **Cambricks & Gloves.** *Another Chest, containing their Beauty washes, Pomatums, l'Eau d'Hongrie, l'Eau de Luce, l'Eau de Carme, &c. &c. &c. near French Wines and Brandies. At a Distance Landing, Swarms of Milliners, Taylors, Mantua-makers, Frisseurs, Tutoresses for Boarding-schools, disguis'd Jesuits, Quacks, Valet de Chambres, &c. &c. &c.*

*Publish'd according to Act of Parliament, March [illegible] [illegible] John Bowles and Son, at the Black Horse in Cornhill, London.* — Price Sixpence.

*Drawn and Engraved by Mr George Cruikshank* *Published June 1 1822 by John Fairburn Broadway Ludgate*

*"Life" among the Connoifseurs: or, Dick Wildfire & his Friends in the Grand Gallery of the Louv[re]*

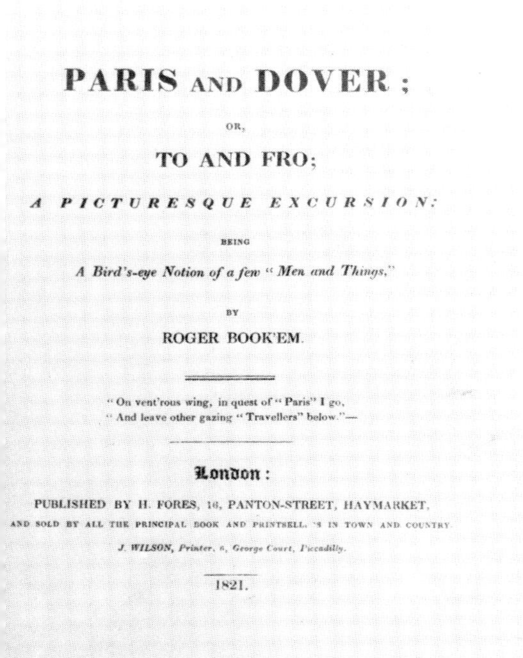

PARIS AND DOVER;

OR,

TO AND FRO;

*A PICTURESQUE EXCURSION:*

BEING

*A Bird's-eye Notion of a few "Men and Things,"*

BY

ROGER BOOK'EM.

"On vent'rous wing, in quest of "Paris" I go,
"And leave other gazing "Travellers" below."—

**London:**

PUBLISHED BY H. FORES, 16, PANTON-STREET, HAYMARKET,
AND SOLD BY ALL THE PRINCIPAL BOOK AND PRINTSELL.'S IN TOWN AND COUNTRY.

*J. WILSON, Printer, 6, George Court, Piccadilly.*

1821.

FAR LEFT Engraving by L. P. Boitard *The Imports of Great Britain from France*, 1757.

FAR LEFT, BELOW George Cruikshank *Life Among the Connoisseurs* or *Dick Wildfire and his friends in the Grand Gallery of the Louvre*, 1822.

LEFT Title page from *Paris and Dover*, 1821.

BELOW *Streets*, plate 15 from *Paris and Dover*.

ABOVE English School *English Milords in Rome*, c. 1749–52.

LEFT John Downman *Sir Ralph Abercrombie (?) with a companion*, 1795–1800.

Mezzotint by William Saye after Sir Joshua Reynolds
*The Society of Dilletanti*, 1821.

Johann Zoffany *Charles Towneley and his friends in the Park Street Gallery, Westminster.*

TOP James Webber *The Resolution beating through the Ice, with the Discovery in the most eminent danger in the distance*, from his *Views in the South Seas*, 1808.

ABOVE, LEFT Tilly Kettle *King of Oudh.*

ABOVE, RIGHT Thomas Phillips *Byron in Albanian Costume.*

# *Public Life*

Men and women in the eighteenth century lived very much more publicly than we do today yet, curiously enough, much more intimately. Members of fashionable clubs such as Brooks's, Whites or Boodles, would know every member, probably knew, indeed, a great deal about his family and his fortune. Today that would be nowhere near true. Similarly, sauntering down Bond Street, window-shopping in the 1770s and 80s or even before, it would be wildly unlikely if one did not run into a lot of people one knew. Again, in Bath or Tunbridge Wells, one was unlikely not to know at least half of the people visiting like oneself. The same was true of the great public resorts of London such as Vauxhall and Ranelagh. In Rome, on the Grand Tour, most of the young English aristocrats not only knew each other but were often related, for the aristocracy was very tightly knit.

This would also have applied to lawyers at the inns of court or prosperous people living in the country towns – in Leicester, Exeter, Chester, Norwich and Bury St Edmunds: society too was closely knit. When one left one's home to go anywhere in one's immediate environment, one was bound to meet friends. Hence public life had an intimacy that is comparatively rare today – though not unknown: at Covent Garden, Glyndebourne, Henley, the royal enclosure at Ascot, or the Oxford and Cambridge match at Lords, the experience is similar. There are still a few, mainly upper-class, festivities that bring friends and acquaintances together in a way that was general and commonplace in the eighteenth century. The world of 'ton' as the eighteenth century called it was quite small, and this had a profound effect on public life. Fashion thrives best in affluent, competitive groups. And fashion in the second half of the eighteenth century became so aggressively extravagant that it, at times, bordered on the absurd – hats that looked like a vegetable stall, hair styles both for men and women of astonishing complexity and idiocy. Women's clothes developed bustles of elephantine proportions whilst men's clothing, favoured by Beau Brummel and the Prince Regent, went the other way – subdued colours and severe lines but most expensively tailored. But these fashions needed to be paraded – hence the popularity of Vauxhall and Ranelagh and the Pantheon, where sauntering, showing off, flirting, was half the pleasure. Probably the same was true of the pleasure gardens and assembly rooms of the provincial towns or the promenades at the spas and the seaside resorts.

It became a golden age for shopkeepers, who learned to entice customers with better designed shops and extensive advertising. Design was important for there was a great deal of profit to be made by anyone who could start a new fashion or give a new and decisive twist to clothes or furnishings. Wherever there are highly fashionable circles, men and women will want to break into them, and others, less affluent, will want to ape the fashions if they can get copies cheaply. And shopkeepers and manufacturers were very eager to exploit the broader market. The late eighteenth century developed new methods, new materials: silver plate, for example, which looks like silver but is much cheaper and so could adorn a lower middle-class table.

However, one needed more than possessions. An exclusive fashionable circle, like a tribe, has many signals shared by those who belong. The signals, or manners, of the Georgian era were elaborate, they had to be learned – even to how one should enter a room, make a bow, hand a lady to dinner. Hence deportment was very important, so was knowledge of the latest dances, or the fashionable activities – watercolours for girls, how to sit well on a horse or shoot, for boys. And this affected education. Dancing and fencing masters were in great demand, a smattering of knowledge of music and French, an insistence on correct deportment and the obliteration of a provincial accent were all highly desirable.

And men and women of the eighteenth century talked. They really believed in conversation – hence the proliferation of clubs like Dr Johnson's. They also believed in knowledge. However, anyone aspiring even to the modest fashionable world of Leeds or Norwich needed education – and a fashionable education too. Small private schools, both for boys and girls, flourished exceedingly: the boys' education was a mixture of utility and polish; the girls' had polish combined with a basic education of reading and writing and a little domestic economy.

Threading through these public activities of the fashionable worlds was a strong spirit of competition, a competition that was deeply involved in *things*, whether it was a new house, a new garden, a new frock, or the smartest educational establishment. The rich and the not so rich no longer feared to parade their wealth and enjoy it.

TOP Antonio Canaletto *Interior of the Rotunda at Ranelagh*, 1743.

ABOVE Thomas Rowlandson *Vauxhall Gardens*, 1784.

TOP Thomas Rowlandson *A Gaming Table at Devonshire House.*

ABOVE Engraving by George Cruikshank *Tom and Jerry, in the Saloon at Covent Garden.*

SPLITFARTHING
The modern Bard says Tom, sublimely sings
Of Virtuous, gracious, good, uxorious Kings,
Who love their Wives so constant from their Hearts
Who down at Windsor daily go a shopping
Their Heads so lovely into Houses popping,
And doing wonders in the haggling Art.
A MILLINER's SHOP.
London Published March 21st 1787 by S W Fores No 3 Piccadilly
And why, in God's name, should not Queens & Kings
Purchase a Comb, or Corkscrew, Lace for Cloaks,
Edging for Caps, or Tape for Apron-Strings,
Or Pins or Bobbin, shop as other Folks,
Reader to make thine Eyes with wonder Stare,
Farthings are not beneath the Royal Care!

LEFT, ABOVE Etching attrib. Henry Kingsbury *A Milliner's Shop*, 1787.

LEFT Thomas Gainsborough *The Mall in St James's Park*.

ABOVE Walking dresses from Heideloff's Gallery of Fashion, 1796.

TOP Arthur Devis *Breaking-up Day at Dr Clayton's School at Salford.*

ABOVE Trade card advertising Sloane House, a boarding school for young ladies, 1797.

# *Sea Water Bathing.*

## MR. LLOYD

RESPECTFULLY informs the Public, the above Vessel (of Forty Tons Burthen, so constructed as to fill herself in the Sea) is constantly kept going to and from the Ocean, to Black-Friar's Bridge; from whence the Water is conveyed to his Baths, in *Bagnio Court, Newgate Street*, and deposited in Reservoirs under Ground.

### TERMS OF BATHING.

**SEA WATER.**

| | L. | S. | D. |
|---|---|---|---|
| Cold Bath, per Month | 1 | 1 | 0 |
| Ditto, Single Time | 0 | 3 | 0 |
| Warm Bath, each Time | 0 | 7 | 6 |
| Or Six Times for | 2 | 2 | 0 |
| *N. B.* Children dipt at | 0 | 1 | 0 |
| Sea Water sold at per Gallon | 0 | 0 | 6 |

**SPRING WATER.**

| | L. | S. | D. |
|---|---|---|---|
| Cold Bath, per Year | 1 | 1 | 0 |
| Ditto, per Month | 0 | 10 | 6 |
| Ditto, single Time | 0 | 2 | 0 |
| Warm Bath, each Time | 0 | 4 | 0 |
| Or Six for | 1 | 1 | 0 |
| Vapour Bath, each | 0 | 5 | 0 |

*Ladies and Gentlemen Cupped at the Baths, or waited on in Town or Country*

BY EXPERIENCED CUPPERS OF BOTH SEXES.

Trade card advertising sea-water baths in Newgate Street, London.

TOP Benjamin West *The Bathing Place at Ramsgate*, c. 1788.

ABOVE Thomas Rowlandson *Treatment at Bath*.

TOP Print of the spa town of Great Malvern, Worcestershire.

ABOVE Anon. *The Ballroom, Scarborough*, 1813.

# Acknowledgments

The publishers have taken all possible care to trace and acknowledge the ownership of all the illustrations. If by chance we have made an incorrect attribution we apologise most sincerely and will be happy to correct the entry in any reprint, provided that we receive notification.

Sources in roman type indicate the owners of paintings and photographs; those in italics refer to illustration sources only.

Arthur Ackermann and Son Limited: *Weidenfeld and Nicolson Archives* 126 (bottom)
Courtesy of Birmingham Public Libraries: *Weidenfeld and Nicolson Archives* 103
Brindsley Ford Collection, London: *Cooper-Bridgeman Library* 67
British Museum, London: 14, 59 (bottom), *Weidenfeld and Nicolson Archives* 75 (bottom), *Weidenfeld and Nicolson Archives* 140 (top); Banks Collection 57 (bottom), 61, 70 (top), 99 (top), 104, 105, 131 (bottom), 135 (bottom), 152 (bottom), 153; Heal Collection 86, 87, 99 (bottom)
Burnley Borough Council, Townley Hall Art Gallery and Museums: 144
Christie, Manson and Wood, London: *Weidenfeld and Nicolson Archives* 65, 152 (top)
Collection of Sir Ian Forbes Leith of Fyvie: 22
*Cooper-Bridgeman Library, London*: 16, 81 (top)
Courtauld Institute of Art, London: 83
Andrew Gifford Collection, London: 90 (bottom)
Glasgow Art Gallery and Museum: 33
Grosvenor Estate: *Cooper Bridgeman Library, London* 127 (bottom)
Guildhall, London: 58 (bottom)
Jockey Club, Newmarket: 42, 114 (bottom), 116 (bottom)
Louvre, Paris: 63
Metropolitan Museum of Art, Dick Fund, 1941, New York: 149 (top)
Marylebone Cricket Club: *Cooper-Bridgeman Library* 122 (top)
Mr and Mrs Paul Mellon Collection, Virginia: 54 (top), 116 (top)
National Gallery, London: 148 (top)
Courtesy of the National Gallery of Ireland, Dublin: 52 (bottom)
National Gallery of Scotland, Edinburgh: 55, 91 (top), 97
National Portrait Gallery, London: 74 (bottom), 84 (top, bottom left and right), By Permission of the Executors of Miss Lloyd-Baker 85, 107, 145 (bottom left)
National Trust, London: 62 (bottom), 64 (bottom)
By Gracious Permission of H.M. the Queen: 91 (bottom)
Royal Academy of Arts, London: 109, Duke of Hamilton Collection, Southill 134 (top), Viscountess Galway Collection 72
Royal Thames Yacht Club, London: *Cooper-Bridgeman Library* 122 (bottom)
Trustees of the Sir John Soane's Museum, London: 56 (top), *Weidenfeld and Nicolson Archives* 75 (top)
Surrey County Library, Epsom: 117
Science Museum, London: 102 (top), 137
Sotheby Parke Bernet, London: 5
South London Art Gallery: *Cooper Bridgeman Library* frontispiece
Tate Gallery, London: 9, 52 (top), 74 (top), 79, 98 (top), 125 (bottom), 126 (top), 142 (bottom), *Cooper-Bridgeman Library* 151
Victoria and Albert Museum, London: 53, 58 (top), *Cooper-Bridgeman Library* 115 (top), 127 (top), 130, 148 (bottom), 149 (bottom)
Viscountess Galway Collection: *Weidenfeld and Nicolson Archives* 78
Walker Art Gallery, Liverpool: 54 (bottom)
*Weidenfeld and Nicolson Archives, London*:

# *Index*

Page numbers in italics refer to illustrations